RHODE ISLAND
MIDDLETOWN
NEWPORT
Fogland Ferry
Grist Mill
Little Sandy Pt.
Mr. Bowler
Mr. Elam
Mr. Lopez
Black Point
Mr. Rome
Mr. Overing
Mr. Jepson
Mr. Gould
Mr. Tillinghast
Thomas Banister
Wm. Redwood
Mr. John Banister
Mr. Dudley
White Hall
Mr. Honyman
Mr. Barker
Charity Farm
Woods Castle
Mr. Walter Easton
Mr. Nicholas Easton
Mr. Jonathan Easton
Eastons Beach
EASTONS BAY
Eastons Point
Sachueast Beach
SACHUEAST BAY
Shooting Rock
Island Rocks
Flint Rock
Sachueast Point
SEAKONNET
Brown's Point
Church's Point
Church's Cove
Cormorant Rock
Gull Rock
Coggeshall's Ledge
Seakonnet Point
Seakonnet Rocks

JAMESTOWN

JAMESTOWN

Architecture, Landscape, and the Making of a Rhode Island Paradise

JOHN R. TSCHIRCH and DAVID E. WEISMAN

David E. Weisman
in association with D Giles Limited

R. 83

Dedication

To those who have dwelled on Jamestown, shaped its land, created its buildings, and preserved its heritage.

Peter Francis Drury. Photo, 1911. Jamestown Historical Society.

Fort *Dumpling*. Photo, ca. 1890. Jamestown Historical Society.

"Entering the harbor, on the left your eye rests upon a small oval fort, gray, time-worn, and dilapidated, standing on the island of Conanicut, and known by the somewhat inexpressive name of 'Dumpling'… . The fort has been left for many years to the corroding tear of the elements, but, while the interior works have been gradually destroyed, the outer walls remain as complete and firm as they ever were … as a picturesque ruin, it has its charms and has become a favorite place of resort for pleasure-parties, who cook their fish and bake their clams on the spot that once resounded to the thunder of artillery. For a century the winds have beat upon the old fort; the Cross of St. George has waved over it; the French fleet swept round it as the vessels moved up to their winter anchorage in the harbor; the Stripes and Stars long ago supplanted the British ensign; it is more venerable than the Republic; and we trust that it will be left undisturbed for ages, as it is one of the few memorials in existence of our early history, and may do something to take away the reproach brought against us by our brethren over the sea that we have no ruins in the United States."

William Cullen Bryant, ed.,
Picturesque America; or, The Land We Live In, 1872

ACKNOWLEDGMENTS

The author thanks the following individuals and organizations for their efforts on behalf of this publication: David Weisman, who brought the vision for the book and continued his support and insight throughout the writing and design process; Charles McGowan, research associate for this project, whose detailed and insightful approach to locating, analyzing, and interpreting historic documents and images rendered invaluable service to each phase of the volume's creation and layout; Rosemary Enright of the Jamestown Historical Society, who graciously worked on the rich collection of period images featured here; Bert Lippincott, who shared his wisdom and knowledge of Jamestown and its history; Sandy Nesbitt, who lent his extraordinary expertise in photography; and the Rhode Island Historical Society and the Pennsylvania Academy of the Fine Arts, who made their collections available, thus enriching the documents and images for this book.

Haystack. Photo, ca. 1920. Jamestown Historical Society.

David E. Weisman, Co-editor

© 2025 John R. Tschirch and David E. Weisman

First published in 2025 by GILES

An imprint of D Giles Limited
66 High Street,
Lewes, BN7 1XG, UK
gilesltd.com

ISBN (hardcover): 978-1-913875-70-1

All rights reserved

No part of the contents of this book may be reproduced, stored in a retrieval system, or transmitted in any form or by any means, electronic, mechanical, photocopying, recording, or otherwise, without the written permission of David E. Weisman, the author, and D Giles Limited.

EU GPSR Authorised Representative:
LOGOS EUROPE, 9 rue Nicolas Poussin, 17000,
LA ROCHELLE, France
E-mail: Contact@logoseurope.eu

For the Client:
Co-editor: David E. Weisman
Project director, author, and co-editor: John R. Tschirch

For D Giles Limited:
Copy-edited and proofread by Sarah Kane
Designed by Matt Wilson
Produced by GILES, an imprint of D Giles Limited

Printed and bound in Europe

MIX
Paper | Supporting responsible forestry
FSC® C118234

Frontispiece: William Trost Richards. *Our Afternoon at Conanicut*. Watercolor on paper, 1878. Courtesy of the Pennsylvania Academy of the Fine Arts. Gift of Dorrance H. Hamilton in memory of Samuel M. V. Hamilton.

pp. 4–5: William Trost Richards. *Joseph Wharton's Harbor in Mackerel Cove*. Watercolor and Chinese white on paper, 1883. Courtesy of the Pennsylvania Academy of the Fine Arts. Gift of Dorrance H. Hamilton in memory of Samuel M. V. Hamilton.

Front and back cover: William Trost Richards. *Mackerel Cove*. Oil on canvas, 1894. Private collection.

CONTENTS

FOREWORD

by David E. Weisman

As is the case in every undertaking of this nature, establishing the theme and core thread that holds a story together is critical. In approaching this book about Jamestown, Rhode Island, our central idea was to describe the special quality of place that is Jamestown and to tell the story of its history, geography and topography, land use, and development in a manner that captures its picturesque beauty. To bring our narrative to life, we wove into it descriptions and images of the Shingle Style architecture together with the romantic paintings of the nineteenth-century landscape artists who resided in and visited Jamestown. We then sprinkled in a mix of tales of the diverse personalities who summered and lived on the island.

I was fortunate to meet John Tschirch when my wife, Jacqui Michel, and I needed his professional assistance working on a historic restoration project in Jamestown. That initial undertaking led to conversations about how each of us defined Jamestown in the history and setting of Rhode Island—and the contrast between the quietness of this place when compared with the "glitter" of its island neighbor, Newport. From those conversations, we both expressed a similar conclusion that Jamestown was "a place apart," and that in our combined knowledge and experience, the uniqueness of Jamestown had not been fully explored or presented in a way that did it justice. From the beginning of our endeavor, I found John to be the perfect guide.

On a personal level, Jamestown was a destination beyond the Narragansett beaches. It was where my father summered as a young camper and then visited while a naval officer during World War II. As a family, my parents would pack us into the car and take day trips to the Narragansett Bay beaches to escape the summer heat of Providence. Even then, Jamestown seemed more of a stopping-off point. Many of its Shingle Style houses were hidden by overgrown greenery or rock ledges, which meant they were best viewed from the water. Later, it also became a summer residence and a marina to sail from. More enduring were the emotional memories instilled in me by the topography of fields in the north and rolling rock ledges and seascape in the south combined with the Shingle Style cottages on the island. These early memories later kindled in me the desire to translate into artistic expressions those emotional guideposts of land, rock, and ocean so as to present Jamestown's special beauty.

To write about Jamestown is to begin with its island life and the fact that for centuries it was only accessible by boat and vessel. It remained this way until 1940 when a bridge, now the Verrazzano Bridge, was built, joining it to the Narragansett mainland to the west. But the ferry was still the only way to reach Newport, until the construction of the Newport Bridge (Claiborne Pell Bridge), in 1969. Even with bridges connecting it to the mainland and Newport, if you asked the majority of Rhode

The Barnacle. Photo, ca. 1915. Jamestown Historical Society.

Islanders and travelers about Jamestown, they would think of it more as a "stopping-off place" than a final destination. This sense of remove helped to preserve the island's special character, defined by a topography of ocean scenery and pastoral meadows, which give meaning and purpose to our rationale and objective for this book.

In the process of researching the history of Jamestown for this project, it became apparent how many significant and often overlooked historical events were linked to it. The Native American heritage, the presence and lives of the enslaved and indentured servants, the burning by the British of Jamestown, and the military significance of the island became markers for the story. Although the book is not intended as an in-depth historical investigation, we hoped to bring into focus moments in Jamestown's history and to highlight their importance in the development of the island.

There are a great many books that portray in text and photographs the Shingle Style architecture of New England, Newport, and Rhode Island, as well as excellent essays and studies of the island and the architecture of Jamestown. However, it was the creative talent of John Tschirch, who proposed combining such a study with his passion for the nineteenth-century American landscape painter William Trost Richards, together with poetry and other artists' work and writings, that turned our book into more than just a compendium of history and architecture. This book provides an integrated perspective on art, culture, and nature as defining factors of Jamestown, reflected in the unique shoreline and topography of the island and the whimsy of houses designed by Charles L. Bevins and others. All is presented in a manner that is intended to capture and convey the romantic, picturesque character of the place. In arriving at this approach, John was well aware of my own involvement in researching and collecting the work of the community of Montmartre artists of the period 1870–1920s that formed the foundation for the birth of modern art. It was therefore easy to understand how John's vision for the story would evolve in its own special way, combining history, architecture, landscape, and painting.

We have included here tales of some of the island's varied personalities and characters. Most of these are founded in historical fact or, in the case of the pirate Captain Kidd, in part interpreted fact and in part legend and folklore. Nonetheless, we hope that the intermix of these individuals brings a degree of revelation, interest, and charm to the reader. Taken together, our goal was to include a portion of their stories so as to present the reader with a context of lives that would bring into the story of Jamestown a number of rich human characters to parallel the physical beauty of the place.

Finally, although Jamestown stands firmly on its own in importance, the discussion of the island inevitably turns to a comparison with Newport, with its better-known historical legacy. It was in fact with full acceptance of the contrast between the secluded scenery and rustic character of Jamestown and the "golden glow" and fashionable polish that is given to Newport, whenever comparisons are made, that we embarked on this book. Jamestown has been and remains in its own right a unique, romantic, and picturesque place not to be overlooked, but to be even more valued for its own natural beauty and history.

I wish to pay special tribute to the work of John Tschirch and the relationship we developed based on his open and willing sharing of ideas, edits, and approaches as we collaborated on this project. His talent was easily recognized from his prior two books on Newport, but the surprise was his readiness to work on a book on Jamestown fully allowing for another person's involvement. I want to thank the excellent team of scholars and experts that worked with John in developing the research for this project.

I also want to acknowledge the role that my parents played in conveying to me the joy and beauty to be found on the Narragansett shore and the appreciation for the Shingle Style houses built along the Rhode Island ocean coastline as well as for the importance of art, poetry, and music in life in addition to the more normal parental lessons of hard work and education. I hope that I have passed on some of those similar teachings to my own children as well.

And finally, I wish to recognize the talent and creativeness of my wife, Jacqui Michel, who has been an important part of this journey in her own right and is a prime contributor to my undertaking of this Jamestown project as well as to so many others during our lives together.

A NOTE FROM THE AUTHOR

by John R. Tschirch

THE SPIRIT OF PLACE AND HOW TOPOGRAPHY and architecture interact to produce something extraordinary provided the inspiration for this book. The idea of paradise pervades the island throughout its history, from the abundant grasses valued by the native Narragansetts, the fattened cattle and sheep raised by European colonizers, and the sublime natural beauty that attracted nineteenth-century summer visitors. William Cullen Bryant's description of Jamestown and the island of Conanicut in *Picturesque America* (1872) reinforced the idea that the land is a defining feature of the place, determining the way people live, work, build, and interpret their setting in a variety of art forms, from architecture to painting and literature. In searching for the character of the island through the ages, it became evident that the rugged coast and pastoral meadows influenced the development of the island's architecture from colonial settlement through the Victorian age and beyond. Buildings appear to emerge out of the soil and rocky terrain and immerse back into these landscape features at the same time. What created this special quality? Why did it happen here? This book endeavors to find out through maps, rare written accounts, paintings, engravings, and an exploration of the place itself, which provides some of the answers, or, at the very least, a particular perspective and way of viewing the island.

View from Sandbeach Cove. Photo, ca. 1890. Jamestown Historical Society.

INTRODUCTION

PASTORAL AND PICTURESQUE; A VISION OF paradise on the Rhode Island coast. These are the defining features of Jamestown, set on Conanicut Island, resting at the entrance to Narragansett Bay. Pastures and orchards roll down to salt marshes in the northern and central portions of the island, and rocky promontories soar above the roiling waves of the Atlantic Ocean to the south. Topography and the sea produce extraordinary scenery, while for centuries builders devised architecture that seamlessly rose from and nestled back into jagged stone coast and gentle meadow. This is an ancient place of timeless natural beauty and time-worn buildings, each a product of the other. The atmosphere is one of removal, of an isolated world within sight of larger islands and the mainland. Within the historical record, the idea of paradise for some did not apply to all. In addition to agricultural abundance and natural beauty, the golden glowing image of paradise had its dark side through the labor of the enslaved who worked the land. History and scenery abound at every turn, and have in turn witnessed and inspired generations to build, plant, paint, write, worship, swim, sail, create, cultivate, and contemplate.

Like a soft mist upon the evening shore,
At once a lovely isle before me lay,
Smooth and with tender verdure covered o'er,
As if just risen from its calm inland bay;
Sloped each way gently to the grassy edge,
And the small waves that dallied with the sedge.
The barley was just reaped—its heavy sheaves
Lay on the stubble field—the tall maize stood
Dark in its summer growth, and shook its leaves—
And bright the sunlight played on the young wood—
For fifty years ago, the old men say,
The Briton hewed their ancient groves away.

William Cullen Bryant,
"A Meditation on Rhode Island Coal," 1840

View from the Porch of the J. B. Sword Cottage. Photo, ca. 1890. Jamestown Historical Society.

This land is loved by ocean; far and deep
The long bays reach among sloping fields;
And tenderly the shining waters creep
Where waiting marsh a silent welcome yields,
And slow brown currents in the shadows run,
And thick-ranked sedges glitter in the sun

Amos Russel Wells,
"Rhode Island," 1921

William Trost Richards. *Looking Toward Mount Hope from Conanicut Island*. Watercolor and Chinese white on paper, 1883. Courtesy of the Pennsylvania Academy of the Fine Arts. Gift of Dorrance H. Hamilton in memory of Samuel M. V. Hamilton.

A PLACE OF CONTRASTS: TOPOGRAPHY

IF HISTORY IS TO BE FULLY ACKNOWLEDGED, one must look beyond recorded time, when retreating glaciers and the convulsions of the earth forced granite to soar high, shifting earth to shape the cliffs, marshes, and meadows of Conanicut (Fig. 1). This great event occurred an estimated two hundred million years ago. Sediments transformed into sandstone, shale, slate, and conglomerate. Not to be left out of this earthly drama, leaves, stems, and trunks of plants imprinted themselves upon the rocks and are still found today.[1] Other thick layers of vegetation evolved into coal deposits, and molten rock deep in the earth infiltrated bands of stone as dramatic white streaks (Fig. 2). Cliffs face open ocean on the southern coast at Beaver Neck, ending in Beavertail Point, taking on the force of the sea and the velocity of wind in this most exposed section of the island. A narrow, low-lying sandy stretch tenuously connects Beaver Neck with the remainder of Conanicut. Mackerel Cove is the main water feature at this juncture of land masses. The topography then rises gently to the north in meadows bordered by the calmer waters of Narragansett Bay (Figs. 3–5). Nine miles long, from north to south, and about one mile at its widest, views of water appear at almost every point.

On the south the Narragansett Basin is partially separated from the sea, at least in those portions of it which are above the water level, by a constriction formed of ancient, highly metamorphosed, stratified rocks and a variety of intrusions, together with some granitic areas which are probably of great age.

N. S. Shaler, "Geology of the Narragansett Basin," *U.S. Geological Survey*, 1899

---

1. Charles Blaskowitz's *Topographical Chart of the Bay of Narraganset*, 1777. Library of Congress. A skilled cartographer, Blaskowitz documented the entire Narragansett Bay region. He noted the abundance of the land, the fine harbors and the important role of islands, such as Conanicut, as key strategic points in the area.

A Topographical CHART of the
BAY of NARRAGANSET in the Province of NEW ENGLAND,
with all the ISLES contained therein, among which
RHODE ISLAND and CONNONICUT
have been particularly SURVEYED,
Shewing the true position & bearings of the Banks, Shoals, Rocks &c. as likewise the Soundings:
To which have been added the several Works & Batteries raised by the Americans.
Taken by Order of the PRINCIPAL FARMERS on Rhode Island.
By CHARLES BLASKOWITZ.
Engraved & Printed for Wm. FADEN, Charing Cross, as the Act directs, July 22d. 1777.
SCALE of Statute Miles.
References to the BATTERIES
A. Providence Fort 50
B. Pappasquash Battery 6 18
C.C. Bristol Ferry Batteries 3 18
D.D. Howlands Ferry Batteries 7
E. Goats Island Fort 25
F. Dyres Point Battery 20
G. Dumpling Rocks Battery 8 18
H. Bristol Battery 8 18
A List of the Principal Farms in RHODE ISLAND.
To the Right Honourable
Hugh Earl Percy,
Baron Percy, Lucy, Poinings, Fitz-Paine, Bryan & Latimer,
Lieutenant General of His Majesty's Forces
in GREAT BRITAIN and AMERICA.
This PLAN is, with his Lordship's Permission,
most humbly Inscribed,
by his most obliged,
devoted & Obedient Servt.
Wm. Faden.
PROVIDENCE RIVER
PROVIDENCE BAY
MOUNT HOPE BAY
BRISTOL BAY
HOG ISLAND
PATIENCE ISLAND
PRUDENCE ISLAND
PORTSMOUTH
RHODE ISLAND
CONNONICUT ISLAND
DUTCH ISLAND
Dighton
Point Peril

2. W. B. Davidson. *Rocks at Fort Wetherill.* Photo, 1895. Jamestown Historical Society. The jagged cliffs and hilly topography of the southern portion of Conanicut, and of coastal Rhode Island in general, is a rare feature in southern New England. The nearby coasts of Connecticut, to the west, and Massachusetts, to the east, are comprised of generally flat expanses of beach. This topographical character includes inlets, marsh, and small valleys, making for a diverse landscape of micro-climates as some areas are exposed to high winds from the ocean, and other sites, sheltered by high stone outcroppings, allowed for the propagation of a variety of plant life.

The shortest distance between Conanicut and Aquidneck, with Newport emerging as its largest city, is at the series of rocky mounds called “The Dumplings,” a landmark feature of the region (Fig. 6). Two nearby islands are also part of Jamestown: 52-acre Gould Island in the East Passage and 111-acre Dutch Island in the West Passage. Together, these three islands form the gateway to the Narragansett Bay basin, often playing a strategic role as military establishments. This topography of contrasts, of jagged stone and fertile meadowlands providing rich grasses, of open storm-tossed coastline and protected coves offering safe harbor, defines the land and determined human settlement patterns through time.

3. William Trost Richards. *The Daisy Field, Conanicut Island*. Watercolor and Chinese white on paper, 1884. Courtesy of the Pennsylvania Academy of the Fine Arts. Gift of Dorrance H. Hamilton in memory of Samuel M. V. Hamilton.

4. *Cottrell Farm.* Photo, ca. 1900. Jamestown Historical Society. A view from the fields to Mackerel Cove.

5. *The Post Windmill.* Photo, ca. 1900. Jamestown Historical Society.

6. *Dumplings*. Charles Blaskowitz's *Topographical Chart of the Bay of Narraganset*, 1777. Library of Congress.

1 *ISLAND REFUGE AND RETREAT: AN HISTORICAL OVERVIEW*

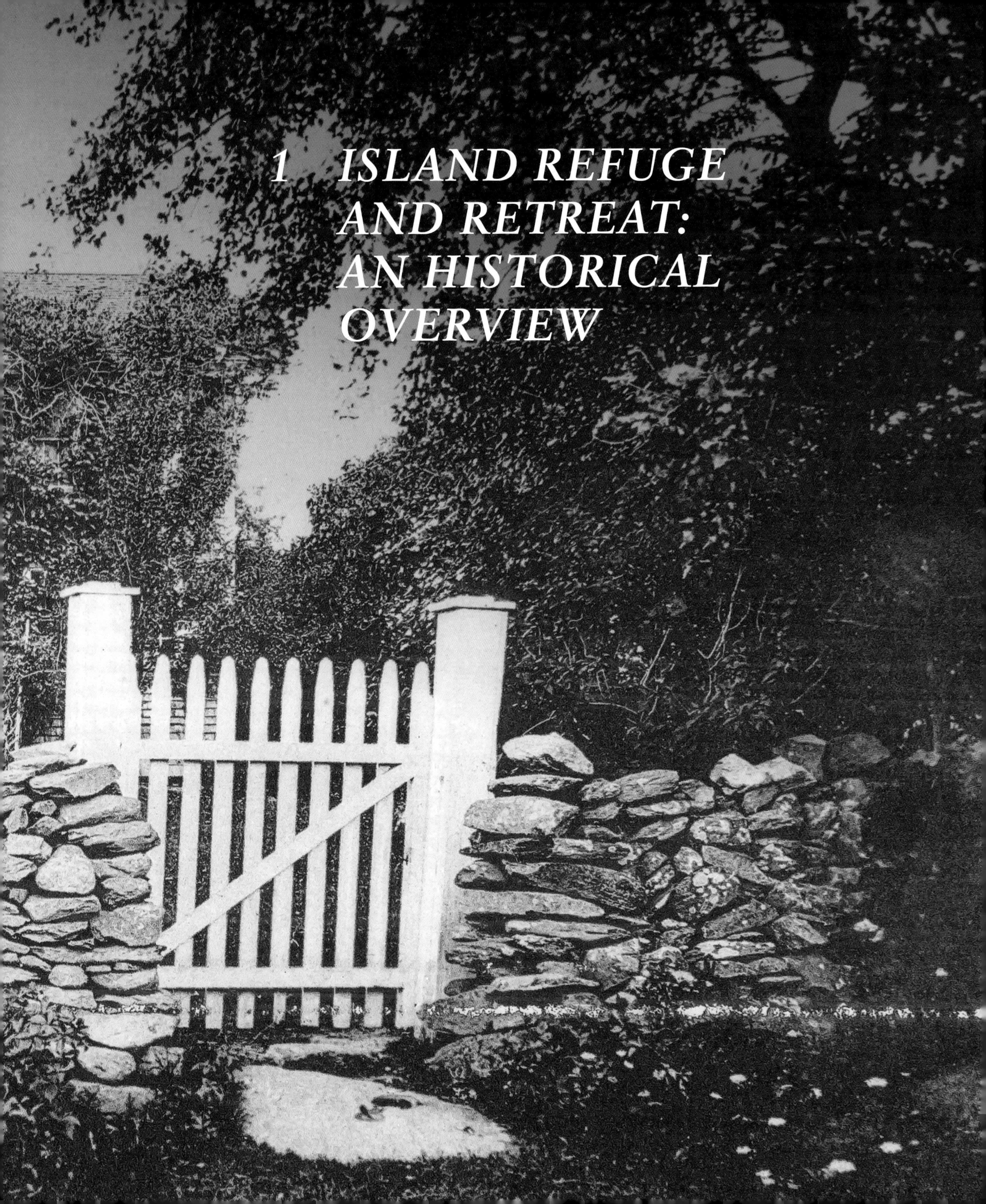

Previous pages: Carr House. Postcard published by Blanchard, Young & Co., Providence, 1907. Jamestown Historical Society.

> *"It would be hard to find elsewhere on our coast an equally limited amount of territory in which are found so many phases of life, so great variety of scenery and so large a fund of legend and history as lie latent or discovered within our own borders."*
>
> Mariana Tallman,
> *Pleasant Places in Rhode Island*, 1893

BY ITS REMOTE NATURE, THE ISLAND OF Conanicut provided protection to its occupants, from the Native Americans forming seasonal encampments here for centuries and the colonial farmers seeking rich grazing lands for sheep to the intrepid Victorians building a seaside escape to indulge their quest for summer retreat and social relaxation. An ancient human presence persists in Native American sites and in the very name of Conanicut, bearing witness to the memory of the Narragansett sachem Conanicus.[2] The land still bears their marks. During their occupation, the Narragansetts systematically burned woodlands in order to clear space for crops.[3] This resulted in rich soil for grasses, which became highly sought after when English settlers appeared on the scene in the seventeenth century. The orderly division of the land into fields and orchards and the simple forms of unadorned farmhouses are testament to the practical organization of the island by colonists for crop production and the raising of sheep and cattle (Fig. 7). Pragmatism directed the development of the seventeenth- and eighteenth-century settlement, while the very opposite impulse—romanticism—created the nineteenth- and early twentieth-century resort, where the picturesque appeal of nature inspired whimsical houses intended to serve the summer escapism of an urban elite. Through the ages, weathered wood and rough-hewn stone characterized farmhouses and resort cottages, telling a story of structures at one with their topographies (Fig. 8). With a cast of characters creating Jamestown, one theme emerges and appears to remain a constant. This island is home to a landscape of cliff, coast, and marshy cove;

7. *Cattle at Hull Cove Farm*. Photo, 1911. Jamestown Historical Society.

8. *Carr Homestead*. Postcard published by Collotype, Elizabeth, N.J. and N.Y, 1949. Sue Maden Postcard Collection. Jamestown Historical Society. The postcard is printed with "built in 1776," indicating the conscious promotion of Conanicut Island's eighteenth-century past. The Carr Homestead became one of the key landmarks of the island's colonial era.

9. William Gilder. *People on Rocks.* Photo, August 1886. Jamestown Historical Society. The arrival of summer visitors in the 1870s and '80s, and their fascination with the picturesque coastline of Conanicut Island, was documented by the new technology of the camera.

10. *Fishermen on Conanicut Avenue.* Photo, 1936. Jamestown Historical Society. Fishermen at the White Nook on Conanicus Avenue.

11. *Benjamin Carr House.* Photo, ca. 1900. Jamestown Historical Society. Demolished in 1910, this shingle-clad, gambrel-roofed house was the type of vernacular structure that inspired the shingled houses of the 1880s such as Stoneseat (see Fig. 12).

12. *Stoneseat.* Photo, ca. 1900. Meredith and Clarke Album. Jamestown Historical Society. Built in 1888 for Admiral Seaton Schroder, the sweeping rooflines of gables and shingled surfaces with no detailed ornament, very much in keeping with earlier rural building traditions on Conanicut Island, is typical of the summer houses of the late nineteenth century.

its buildings a testament to those who sought their fortunes and fulfilled their fantasies, within sight of the mainland, but a world apart (Figs. 9–14). In each case, there is a seamless relationship between the island's topography and its architecture. This is the essence of Conanicut, its special quality, its role as a picture of history in a picturesque place.

13. *Stornaway*. Photo, ca. 1895. Jamestown Historical Society. The B. H. Shoemaker cottage (1883) is attributed to architect Charles L. Bevins and builder J. D. Johnston, each playing a major role in shaping the appearance of Conanicut as a summer resort, specifically in the southern portion of the island, known as Ocean Highlands, and its environs. Stornaway literally nestles in the cliffs, a distinctive aspect of the resort where topography and architecture work in unison.

14. *Hazard Farm*. Photo, 1921. Lena Clarke Album. Jamestown Historical Society. Agricultural life coexisted with resort life on nineteenth- and early twentieth-century Conanicut Island.

2 A BOUNTIFUL LAND: THE NARRAGANSETTS AND COLONIAL SETTLEMENT

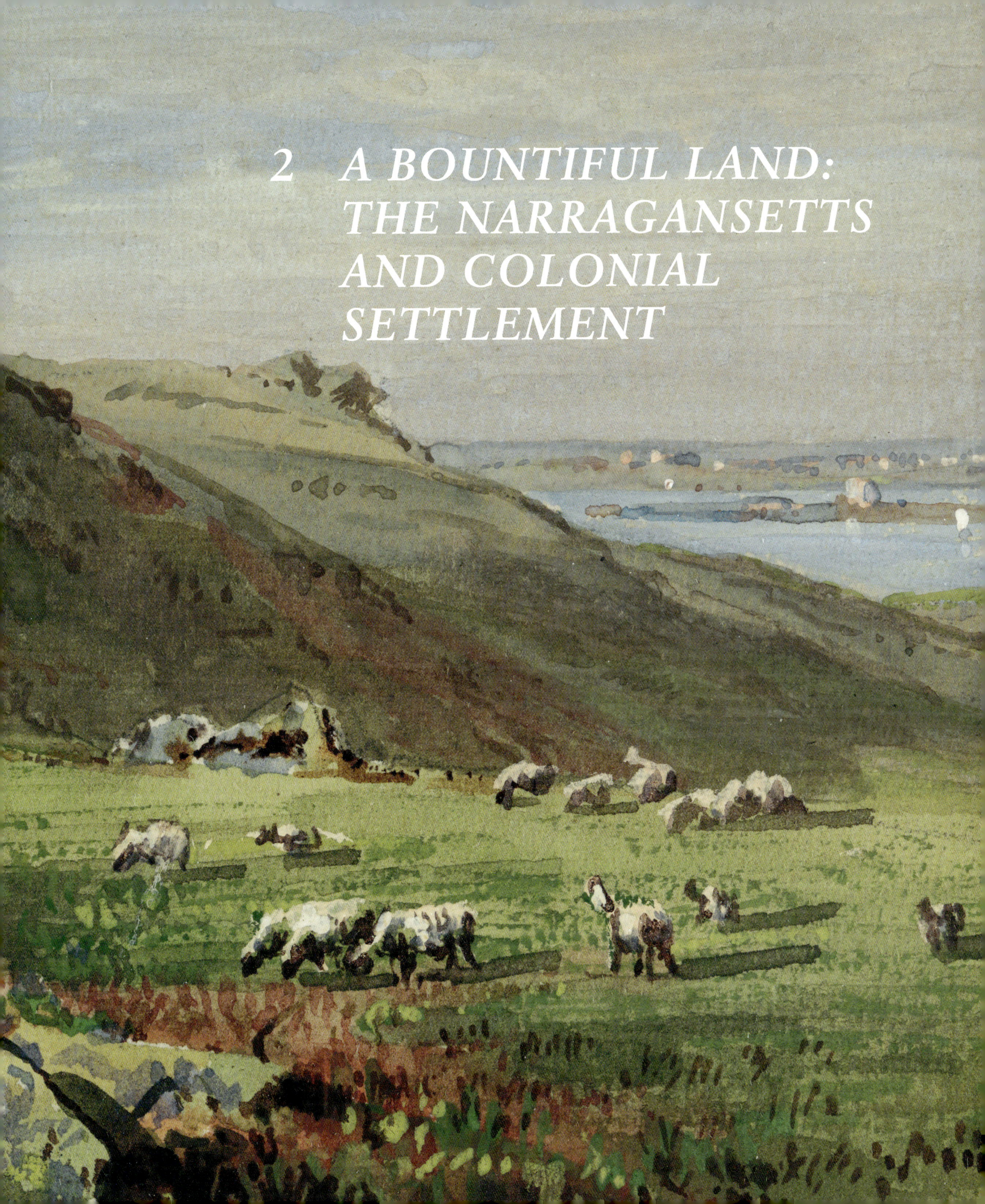

Previous pages: William Trost Richards. *The Sheep Pasture, Conanicut Island.* Watercolor and Chinese white on paper, 1884. Courtesy of the Pennsylvania Academy of the Fine Arts. Gift of Dorrance H. Hamilton in memory of Samuel M. V. Hamilton.

"The Horses ... are strong, the Meat Cattle and Sheep are much the largest in America, the Butter and Cheese excellent, and every necessary of Life in Abundance."

Charles Blaskowitz, *A Topographical Chart of the Bay of Narraganset*, 1777

THE NARRAGANSETTS HAD DWELLED on Conanicut, in the words of the sachem Pressicus, since "time out of mind," cultivating corn and beans and clearing forests through their traditional burning techniques, producing rich grasslands.[4] Conanicut is the site of one of the oldest Native American communities in New England, with evidence of a village and burials dating back over 4,500 years. The Joyner Archaeological Site contains the remains of circular wigwams, fire pits, trash pits, cutting implements fashioned from white quartz and argillite, tools for grinding nuts and seeds, hearths with the remains of deer and passenger pigeon, as well as stored caches of finished tools, paint stones, and other objects of village life. The largest documented Native American burial place in New England is located in the Jamestown Archaeological District, and the modern village has grown up around and within this sacred site.

The first European record of Conanicut appeared in 1524 when Giovanni da Verrazzano wrote his observations in a letter to Francis I, King of France, the sponsor of the exploratory journey of the North American coast from present-day Cape Hatteras to Nova Scotia. As the ship *La Dauphine* entered Port Refuge, later to be named Narragansett Bay, Verrazzano noted the features of present-day Newport, Conanicut, Dutch, and Gould Islands, taking stock of the topography of the region, its rich potential, and its strategic significance (Fig. 15).[5]

15. *Conanicut Island*. Detail from Charles Blaskowitz's *Topographical Chart of the Bay of Narraganset*, 1777. This detail illustrates the division of lands and the trees planted to shade the methodically laid out road systems vital for the transport of agricultural products and the movement of livestock.

In this bay there are five small islands, very fertile and beautiful, full of tall spreading trees, and any large fleet could ride safely among them without fear of tempest or other dangers. Then, going southward to the entrance of the harbor, there are very pleasant hills on either side, with many streams of clear water flowing from the high land into the sea. In the middle of this estuary there is a rock of "viva pietra" [a nonporous rock] formed by nature, which is suitable for building any kind of machine or bulwark for the defense of the harbor.[6] *All this land or New World which we have described above is joined together, but is not linked with Asia or Africa (we know this for certain)… .*

In the ship Dauphine *on the VIII day of July. M.D. XXIIII. Humble servant JANUS VERAZANUS.*[7]

Not only land and sea occupied Verrazzano, but the nature of the population, who came to greet his ship. In his writing, there is a consistent emphasis on imposing, consciously or not, a classical European sensibility on the place and its inhabitants. References to the Narragansetts bearing a resemblance to ancient Egyptians, Syrians, Greeks, and Romans suffuse his prose, even though he would never have first-hand experience of these lost civilizations. It was the first, but not the last, time European cultural ideas would be imposed upon Conanicut. Of the Narragansett greeting committee, Verrazzano stated,

Among them were two kings, who were as beautiful of stature and build as I can possibly describe… . These people are the most beautiful and have the most civil customs that we have found on this voyage. They are taller than we are; they are a bronze color, some tending more toward whiteness, others to a tawny color; the face is clear-cut; the hair is long and black, and they take great pains to decorate it; the eyes are black and alert, and their manner is sweet and gentle, very like the manner of the ancients… . They live on the same food as the other people (which they produce with more systematic cultivation than the other tribes, and when sewing they observe the influence of the moon, the rising of the Pleiades, and many other customs derived from the ancients), and otherwise on game and fish. They live a long time, and rarely fall sick; if they are wounded, they cure themselves with fire without medicine; their end comes with old age. We consider them very compassionate and charitable toward their relatives, for they make great lamentations in times of adversity, recalling in their grief all their past happiness… .[8]

Giovanni da Verrazzano sailed onwards in *La Dauphine*, leaving no settlement. In the early 1600s, Dutch explorers from their base in New Amsterdam made contact on the Rhode Island coast, trading with Native Americans, primarily the Wampanoags in northern Narragansett Bay at the Warren River.[9] Adrian Block sighted Block Island in 1614, and, later, Abraham Pietersen, on behalf of the West India Company, purchased the island of Quentettis, now Dutch Island, off the coast of Conanicut, as a trading post. It would be the English, however, who made a lasting impact on the region, and Conanicut, when Roger Williams, founder of the colony of Rhode Island, gained permission in 1638 for colonists to, "reap the grasses on Conanicut Island" from the sachems Conanicus and Miantonomi.[10] The lure of these grasses is evident in the first meeting of the newly founded town of nearby Newport in 1639.

> *It is agreed and ordered, that the Plantation now begun at this Southwest end of the island shall be called Newport; and that all the landes lying Northward and Eastward from the said Towne ... so across from sea to sea with all ye landes Southward and Westward ... together with the small Islands and the grass of Cunnunnegott, is appointed for the accommodation of ye said Towne.*[11]

Over time, controversy arose when the sachems Scuttop and Quequaquenuit asserted that only the right to use, not own, the grasses had been granted to the colonists. Misunderstanding and distrust emerged with these differing views on land use. In 1656, an entry in the Newport Land Evidence Book recorded,

> *For as much as it is frequently declared that of late there have been endeavors used by some who are neither inhabitants of this Island or members of this Colony, to get into their possession and power of disposal the above Island of Quononaqutt. And considering how commodiously ye said Island lieth for the enlarging the accommodations of some of us, in regard to the nearness of it to our dwellings as also considering the great straight that many of us are in, for want of commonage for cattle, Therefore and for the preventing any foreigners getting into their possession whereby inconvenience and disturbance, yea and probably arise to ye Government of this Colony.*[12]

In 1656, colonists from Newport decided to resolve the issue and establish official ownership of Conanicut. Led by William Coddington and Benedict Arnold, a group of more than one hundred men agreed to purchase Conanicut Island and in 1657 acquired the deed, along with Dutch Island, from Cashanaquont, then the chief sachem of the Narragansetts.[13] Thomas Gould took over the nearby island, which would bear his name, from the sachem Koshtosh in the same year. With colonial European occupation and displacement of Native Americans of Conanicut came a program of private property and land organization. Joshua Fisher surveyed the island and devised a plan whereby 4,800 acres, out of a total of 6,000 acres, were allotted to the proprietors with specific acreage assigned based on the size of each person's investment. Each proprietor also received a plot of land in the proposed village (Figs. 16–20). Benedict Arnold, Sr. ranked as the largest landowner, with over 1,400 acres on the southern end of the island. William Brenton, Roger and Caleb Carr, and William Coddington also held extensive tracts.[14] This ordered settlement of the island can justly be called corporate colonialism, funded by a wealthy power elite from Newport working in concert with very specific goals for raising sheep and other livestock, which evolved as such a lucrative enterprise that a shield with a green field and a silver sheep became the town seal. Two hundred and sixty acres formed the plat for the future town with house lots, mostly of one acre and some larger depending on the amount of overall acreage owned by a proprietor, and twenty acres for an artillery, a burial ground, and a prison house. On April 17, 1657 (recorded on

16. *Underwood Farm*. Photo, 1921. Lena Clarke Album. Jamestown Historical Society.

17. *John Jay Watson Farm*. Photo, 1921. Lena Clarke Album. Jamestown Historical Society. Probably built in 1800 by Burton Watson, son of Job Watson who was styled "King of Conanicut" for his large landholdings. The Watsons would remain prominent figures on Conanicut, responsible for the development of large tracts of land for summer house construction in the late nineteenth and early twentieth centuries. The house is grand by Conanicut standards, featuring a classical pediment over the front door. This is a rarity for the island; most of its eighteenth- and early nineteenth-century dwellings are devoid of any decorative details.

18. *Hazard Farmhouse*. Photo, 1921. Lena Clarke Album. Jamestown Historical Society. The core of the house, built in 1760, has the typical square form with a central chimney. Later additions include a wing (left side of photo) and a mid-nineteenth-century entrance enclosure. Occupied by generations of Carrs, and then generations of Hazards, this colonial era landmark house burned down in December of 2007. A note in the album for this photo reads, "The Hazard Farm. This house stands on the south side of Cemetery Lane beyond the Cemetery. In olden times the lane extended to the west shore where a ferry was located. As near as I can find out, Thomas Hazard, son of Jeremiah Hazard of North Kingston, came to Jamestown and purchased the farm about 1783."

19. *Samuel Carr House*. Photo, ca. 1900. Covell Collection. Jamestown Historical Society. The stone wing is said to be late seventeenth century, with a later wooden addition. Stone buildings in Rhode Island are rare.

20. *Peter and John Howland at Hammond Farm.* Photo, ca. 1920. Jamestown Historical Society. The Howlands are using a hay rake, testament to the central place of hay in the island economy from the colonial period through the early twentieth century.

January 25, 1680 by John Fones Clerk in Newport) the proprietors of Conanicut received the signed deed as follows,

> *Know to all men by these presents that I Cashanaquont and a Chief Sachem and Commander of the Indians of Narragansett Bay and Quononaqutt Island in Narragansett Bay aforesaid, etc. For and in consideration of several gifts of value beforehand received, and also for and in consideration of ye full and just sum of one hundred pounds Sterling … make lawful sale of all and every part and parcel of the aforenamed Island Quononaqutt… . I do engage upon my own proper charges to remove all ye Indian inhabitants, and clear them off from ye aforesaid Island Quononaqutt, and cause them to leave free and full possession of the said Island wholly to ye said purchasers, without putting ye said purchasers to any further charges, either for the Indian Corn Fields or any other labours of theirs that is to remain on said Island at their departure… .*[15]

The sachem Cashanaquont made his mark, and one hundred proprietors signed their names. In addition to the transfer of ownership, the details of the deed established rules for colonial disposition of land, including the final distribution of farm acreage, lots in the village center, the laying out of a north–south main road four rods in width and an east–west road two rods in width, and the use of Dutch Island for common pasturage.[16] In 1678 came the official incorporation as "Jamestown," named in honor of His Royal Highness Prince James, Duke of York, later King James II.[17] Order and accountability ruled in the evolution of the land. The laying out of the island's roads remained a priority, and the responsibility of proprietors to adhere to the agreements of their deeds required proper enforcement. In 1705, the colony's general assembly empowered Jamestown's sheriff, William Coddington, assisted by Captain Joseph Sheffield, to "do with all convenient speed ... see that the aforesaid Highways be laid out or open according to the Plat or Draught... . It is further ordered that Mr. John Mumford be appointed to the Sheriff and Justices with the aforesaid Plat... . And it is further enacted that the Proprietors of Jamestown will pay the whole charge."[18]

By the mid-eighteenth century, the population totaled 556, including 130 Africans, both enslaved and free, and thirty-two Native Americans.[19] A degree of religious diversity prevailed since Roger Williams founded the colony of Rhode Island on the principle of freedom of conscience. Jamestown's largest landholder, Benedict Arnold, served as governor in 1660 when King Charles II signed the colonial charter codifying freedom of worship into law.[20] As a result, Quakers, often persecuted in England and its North American colonies, settled in great numbers. They built their first meeting house in 1710. As the island grew in prosperity, the harbor at the southeastern shore evolved as the location for a ferry and the shipping of exports. This would also become the main ferry point for traffic to Newport, a role maintained for over three centuries until the opening of Newport Bridge in 1969.

21. *Friends Meeting House, Interior*. Photo, ca. 1940. Jamestown Historical Society. Built in 1786, following the destruction of the meeting house as a result of the British occupation of Conanicut during the War for Independence, the architecture and interior features express the Quaker principle of plainness, in one's surroundings as well as in dress, actions, and in speech.

The Case of Remembrance

NATIVE POPULATIONS HELD AN UNSTABLE position in the European-colonized "New World" of the Americas, envisioned as a paradise for the colonizers but a prison for the enslaved and indentured. In Rhode Island, the effects of the conflict known as "King Philip's War" had profound effects upon the Narragansetts. Defeated in the Great Swamp Battle of southwestern Rhode Island, those natives who survived annihilation were enslaved and sent to the Caribbean, while others were remanded into indentured servitude. This practice, involving both European settlers and Native Americans, provided both opportunities for some and virtual enslavement for others. It allowed for Britons to achieve paid passage to the American colonies in return for a number of years of service to a sponsor. Indentured servitude also had its darker side which could result in a lifetime of economic dependence and enforced labor. In 1741, the Town Council ruled on the issue of a Native American youth named Remembrance:

> *Where as Benjamin Sheffield haveing Complaining to the Council that Indian Antony and his Squaw Content and Daughter Remembrance Being Destitute of Sustinance, Voted an act by this Council that ye said Council give Indenture of a Sartan Indian Gall Called Remembrance, Daughter of Indian Antony and his former Squaw Content unto Ebenezer Slocum and his wife Mary and Untall [until] she arrive unto the age of Eighteen years in a common form of Apprentice.*[21]

No account exists of how Antony, Content, or Remembrance might have thought about their economic status or how they felt about the circumstance of indenture. The Town Council defined their situation in European terms and devised a solution that may have appeared practical to them. However, Europeans and Britons generally volunteered for indenture, with the exception of those indentured for penal offenses, while Native Americans were ordered into that situation if they were not deemed financially self-sufficient.[22] There is one record in the Town Council minutes of 1745 that reveals all was not well:

> *... whereas the said Ebenezer Slocum made complaint to this present Council, that the said Girl hath absented herself from his Service. He therefore prays that the said Girl may be bound to him according to said order of the Council. It is therefore resolved that the said Girl be forthwith bound to said Ebenezer and Mary Slocum, and with them to service till she arrive at the Age of Eighteen Years. In Consideration of which service, the said Slocum, shall provide all things needful & necessary for such an apprentice. And that when she Shall compleat her Servitude, the said Slocum, shall give to the said Girl, one Suit of wearing Apparel worth Ten pounds besides her common wearing cloths, And the Clerk of the Council is ordered to sign the Indenture.*[23]

The case of Content and Remembrance illustrates the situation of Native Americans on the island, a product of the European imposition of social order, the manner of making a living, and the place of people depending upon race and economic power. Indentured servitude disempowered and disenfranchised native peoples. Forced labor, whether imposed indentured servitude or direct enslavement, was a major factor in Jamestown's agricultural life. Enslaved Africans and African Americans serving as farm laborers and domestic workers on Conanicut were legally treated as property, part of the brutal economic life of colonial Rhode Island, and the Americas at large, specifically with Newport merchant links with the transatlantic slave trade. According to the census records of 1730 and 1775, the enslaved accounted for one third of the population, and prominent landowners and political leaders, including the Carr, Eldred, Hazard, Underwood, and Weeden families, each held four to five enslaved people, bequeathing these individuals to their descendants in wills along with buildings, fields, household objects, and silver. Over a third of the population of eighteenth-century Jamestown was enslaved Africans or Native Americans subject to enforced indenture. They played a critical role as laborers, shaping the land and producing its agricultural wealth.

The evidence of the bondage of the enslaved in Jamestown is clear in written records. In 1775, the so-called "partial emancipation," which was, in fact, still enslavement, of an enslaved girl named Jane by Damaris Fowler, a widow living in Jamestown, is a testament to the island's treatment of humans as property. Fowler noted that the emancipation would take place when Jane turned eighteen in two years. The document only renounced the one-third of Jane that was owned by Fowler. Others who could have claimed ownership of Jane are not identified, but the record does include the signatures of Mary Callender, Elizabeth Mott, and Ann Smith as witnesses, so they may have been among those who had rights to Jane's person.[24] The fact remained that Jane was not free, but tied to her enslavers.

January 3, 1859 is a poignant moment in the history of Conanicut with the passing of James Howland. Enslaved by the Howlands of Jamestown, he continued to work for the family after his emancipation by the state of Rhode Island. The death certificate recorded James as a single man, a laborer, and of African parentage. Written by hand in the margin is the notation "The last slave of Rhode Island freed under the act of 1792." There are few specific buildings or monuments to fully acknowledge the presence of enslaved Africans and African Americans on Conanicut, but they survive on paper, and it is through census records, emancipation documents, and death notices that their existence is recognized and their status defined. The land itself also stands as a record, its fields and stone walls created, in part, by them, during the colonial period and thereafter, in which they were a major presence in the shaping of the island.

22. *Windmill Door* (detail). Photo, mid-twentieth century. Merrill Smith Collection. Jamestown Historical Society. Simple, straightforward construction, weatherworn, this image of the windmill door encapsulates the story of Jamestown's buildings, made of sturdy materials, showing the effects of time.

With an island economy based on agricultural production, the enslaved labored in eternal servitude and the indentured worked primarily in farm and field, living under the control of Town Council orders in an otherwise bountiful land noted for its grasses, grains, and the export of its fine livestock. Isolated in the bay from natural predators, Conanicut provided superb terrain for raising sheep, cows, hogs, and horses. As early as the 1680s, domesticated animals appeared to dominate in the landscape, so much so that new regulations attempted to monitor their movement and the conduct of their human owners: "... no hog nor hogs, no pig nor pigs shall be keep in the highways without a yoak on them."[25] By 1717, the council voted to prohibit pasturing of cattle in the highway, "except young stock under one year old" and ordered that a pound "35 feet long and 25 feet Broad be made in this town" and fines for violation of this order amounted to "2 pence for every Sheep and 6 pence per head for every horse or mair with all charges of poundage."[26]

Agriculture dictated not only the organization of land but also the types of buildings created to serve that enterprise in terms of forms and materials. Weather and wood determined the shape and physical orientation of early farmhouses, sturdy cubes secured with large corner timbers, exterior walls sheathed in shingles, and main facades facing south to capture sunlight. In this manner, Jamestown's builders followed the pattern of much of rural New England (Figs. 22–27). While no seventeenth-century structures survive in unaltered form, and many colonial era houses were destroyed during the War for Independence, the buildings that do still stand provide a window onto a world where a focus on utility resulted in architectural solidity and beauty.

One instance in particular has both sacred and profane meanings. Joseph Greene, among the earliest colonizers to develop his land, planted hay-seed and constructed a dwelling, which his descendant, also named Joseph, gave to the Society of Friends in his will, declaring, "My farm on the Island of Conanicut

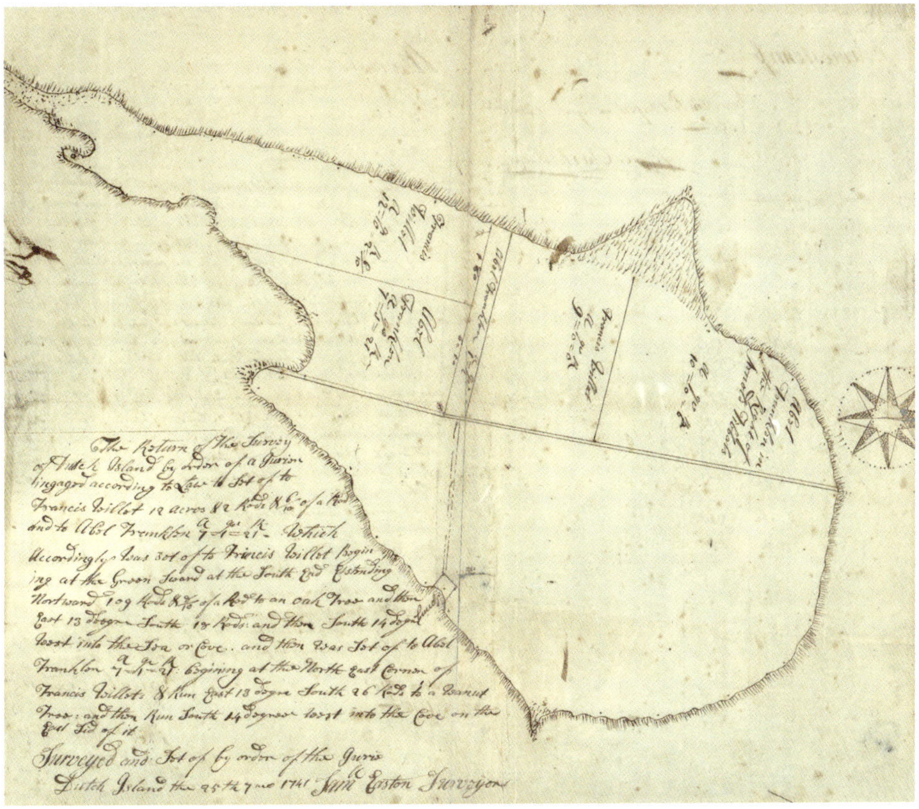

23. *Survey of Dutch Island with Division of Lands*, 1741. Jamestown Historical Society.

24. *Sheep Shearing at the John Jay Watson Farm*. Photo, 1921. Jamestown Historical Society. Sheep, along with other livestock, were the foundation of Conanicut Island's agricultural economy from colonial settlement through the early twentieth century. The number of livestock reached its zenith in the period 1700–75. It diminished severely during the War for Independence and rebounded in the early nineteenth century, although never reaching its eighteenth-century scale.

25. *Friends Meeting House*. Photo, ca. 1910. Jamestown Historical Society. Mr. and Mrs. Samuel Emlen at the Friends Meeting House. A note in the album states that they might also be Mr. and Mrs. George Emlen. A key point of the photo is that the couple is not in period costume, but in simple attire in the Quaker tradition. The rectangular form with entrances for both genders, given equal standing in the Society of Friends, is an archetypical example of Quaker meeting houses.

26. Hugh L. Taylor. *Windmill*. Photo, 1927. Jamestown Historical Society.

Like the Friend's Meeting house, its neighbor there,
The mill still stands upon its hill site fair,
As if to watch the boats that glide alway
O'er the blue waves of Narragansett Bay,
Free from the pressure of vain-glorious strife.
Type of the truly grand—the simple life.

Maud Lyman Stevens, *The Jamestown Windmill*, 1916

27. *Underwood Farm Apple Trees*. Photo, 1921. Lena Clarke Album. Jamestown Historical Society.

known by the name of Greene Farm, and home thereon standing in which I now live (where my predecessors of the same name lived for generations back, if not from the first settlement of the Island by English Emigrants)."[27] Joseph's high-minded ideals for supporting the Friends speaks of spiritual motives, yet the family contested the will, winning back the farm and retaining it for centuries until they sold it in the early twentieth century for the development of affluent Shoreby Hill.[28]

Although the Friends did not retain the gift of Joseph Greene, in 1684 they did receive approval from the Society of Friends in Newport for a quarterly meeting at the house of Nicholas Carr.[29] By 1709, a separate meeting house became a reality, with the minutes of the Newport Friends' meeting of June 9, 1709 giving "leave for the Friends of Jamestown to build a meeting house on their island."[30] Ebenezer Slocombe deeded land "on which a meeting house stands where the people called Quakers are won't to worship," and a structure rose on the site in 1710.[31] Damaged by the British in 1776, the Friends rebuilt the meeting house in 1786 (see Fig. 21).[32] The one-story wood structure with two entrances and shuttered windows expressed the Friends' testimony of simplicity, their ideal of plainness in speech, dress, and in all material matters. Although clearly articulated by the Friends, a minimalist quality defined eighteenth-century architecture in Jamestown regardless of religious belief, social hierarchy, or financial means (Fig. 25).

The Samuel Carr House, part fieldstone and part wood, offers up an architectural mystery (see Fig. 19). It is possible that the stone section may have been the town prison, but that is mere conjecture. What is true is the fact that stone buildings are rare in colonial Rhode Island due to the lack of lime deposits to make high-grade mortar. Shell mortars made locally were inferior and prevented the creation of large-scale stone architecture. Dwellings were typically shingled cubes with central chimneys. Main facades faced south to take advantage of daylight. Interest in English colonial settlement of Jamestown and the rise of camera technology by the mid-1900s created a legacy of invaluable visual and written documents on the architecture of Conanicut and provided sound evidence of a building tradition dictated by and adapted to the island setting.

With its location on the sea, the colonists harnessed the power of wind and weather to their benefit. On August 4, 1730, the quarterly meeting of the town declared, "Nicholas Carr shall have ye mill that is erected on Jamestown at ye Publick Charge of the Town for his own proper Estate for Ever. He ye S'd Nicholas Carr Paying the Sum of fifty pounds in to the Town Treasury, and be obliged to keep S'd mill in good Repair and during ye terme of Twenty Years."[33] The windmill, sited near present-day Windmill Hill, appeared to be gone by the 1760s, and a new mill was built in 1787, which operated until 1876.[34]

While most buildings addressed the needs of farm and field, the Thomas Paine House directs itself to the sea. Located at present-day East Shore Road, this facade faces the waters of the East Passage of Narragansett Bay and Newport Harbor. Thomas Paine led a life of adventure on the high seas, at times hailed as a hero and at others branded a criminal. He needed to have a clear view of the coast and its privateers, pirates, and patrolling British ships. The waters of Narragansett Bay offered safe haven for a number of officially, and often not officially, sanctioned privateers, directed by the British authorities to prey on enemy vessels in the ongoing struggles and power plays of colonizing European imperialists. Paine's house features a second-floor overhang, seen on seventeenth-century houses in New England, but the only surviving one in Jamestown. In a sketch of 1882, the elaborate central chimney, the overhang, and the shingled facades are evident (see Fig. 131). Thomas Paine did not linger long at his house with its fine vistas from the shoreline. Service to the British Crown beckoned. He was summoned with all fanfare and a flourish of words as follows by Sir Thomas Lynch, Knight, one of the gentlemen of His Majesty's bed chamber, and Captain General in Chief of His Majesty's Island of Jamaica and territories thereon depending; and Vice Admiral to His Royal Highness, James, Duke of York, in the American seas. The man of many titles worded Paine's commission as follows,

> *Whereas I am informed there are several pirates that have barbarously murthered [murdered] divers of His Majesty's subjects, robbed others and taken several vessels, cursing the King, and not so much as pretending to belong to any Prince, or to have any commission of war—These are therefore to authorize Capt. Thomas Paine, commander of the Frigate Pearl, to seize the said pirates, and to take, kill and destroy the said pirates and their ships… . Given under my hand, the 13th October 1682. Jamaica.*
>
> *Signed Thomas Lynch*
> *By His Excellency Commanding*[35]

With the conclusion of hostilities, Captain Paine continued to privateer, and, since his warrant had expired, he at once became labeled a pirate. Lord Bellomont in 1699 made a journal entry, "I also examined Thomas Paine (formerly a pirate) upon his oath, relating to goods or treasure, imported by Capt'n William Kidd, and reported to be left by Kidd with said Paine."[36] Thomas Paine's house, like the man himself, is a survivor, prevailing through war, storms and the more mundane, but significant, intervention of remodeling. Today, it is known as Cajacet, with a picturesquely complex reinterpretation of shingled facades from the 1880s.

A more pastoral and peaceful story prevails at the Carr Homestead, where history and romance appear to co-exist with ease. Caleb Carr, among the original proprietors of Conanicut and governor of the Rhode Island colony in 1695, never lived on the island, instead giving his son Nicholas the property in his will.[37] Nicholas most likely built the house, a wood-shingled structure of solid proportions with simple framing of doors and windows, and a large chimney occupied the center of the structure. No columns or triangular pediments inspired by ancient temples, so fashionable in Georgian houses, appear in Carr's front door, which is an example of rural simplicity. No flights of eighteenth-century architectural fancy embellish the houses of Conanicut.[38] The historic character of the solid simple house is evident in the words of Harry Carr, a journalist given an honorable mention by the Pulitzer Prize Committee of 1934, a columnist for the *Los Angeles Times*, and a direct Carr descendant who stayed in the family homestead in 1925. In his column for the *Times*, he mused on this great-great-grandmother and her still-noticeable presence in the well-preserved house and its objects,

> *Jamestown (R.I.) Sept. 20... . I am writing this in the bedroom of the old colonial farmhouse where she came as a young bride—and in which she died. My great-grandfather must have been a beau; for in the bedroom hangs an old "courting mirror," such as the young dandies used to carry in wooden cases in their saddle-bags, whereby to arrange their wigs when they went a-wooing... . The old farmhouse was already one hundred and twenty years old when Mary came there as a bride... . Up in the old garret I found her old spinning wheel and her old linen wheel ... and the candle molds into which she poured the tallow for the winter lights... . She died on Christmas Eve (1822).*[39]

With the keen eye of the journalist for detail and the personal sentiments of a family member, Harry Carr leaves a clear picture of a house and its objects from times past (see Fig. 19). Weathered and time-worn, the colonial era houses of Conanicut like the Carr Homestead settled into their soil as the eighteenth century progressed, but the peace of their surroundings was never assured. Historical forces came to call, even at quiet places like Conanicut, in the guise of a revolution.

L'Escadre françoise entrant dans Newport sous le feu des Batteries
passèrent sur l'Isle & R

La Ville de Newport.

Batteries sur Rode Island faisant feu sur les Vaisseaux.

Batteries sur Goat Island faisant feu sur les Vaisseaux.

D Isle de Conanicut.

E Vaisseaux françois forçant le passage.

F Vaisseaux François tournant ou qui ont tourne l'Isle de Conanicut.

G Batiments Anglois en feu.

N^ta. Les Anglois brulerent ou coulerent a Rode Island, les Frégates l'Orphée, l
grand nombre de Batiments Marchands.

3 REVOLUTION: AN ISLAND EXPOSED

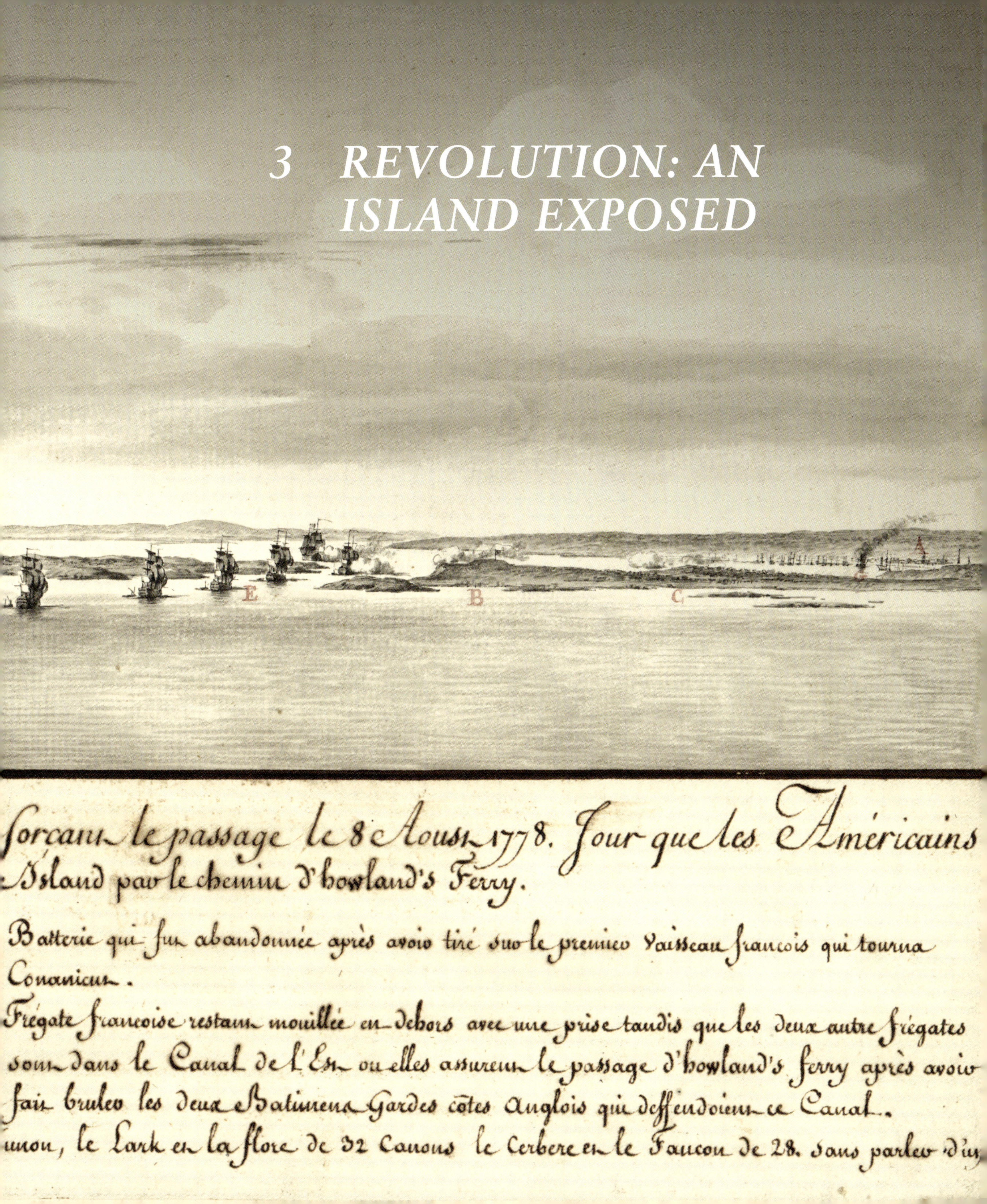

Previous pages: *French Warships in Narragansett Bay*. Map, ca. 1780. Library of Congress.

"The Kings forces fired on Mr. Jno. Martin aet 80 standing at his Door and wounded him Badly. Mr. Fowler had about 30 Head Cattle: these the Regulars carried off and perhaps a dozen Head more, about 30 Sheep & as many Turkeys, & some Hogs, Beds, Furniture and other plunder."

The Literary Diary of Ezra Stiles,
December 11, 1775

ARMIES AND NAVIES ON THE MOVE, the requisition of much-needed supplies, and the strategic location of Conanicut made it a key point for the defensive and offensive campaigns waged in Narragansett Bay during the War for Independence. The small rural population of Jamestown and the island's open meadows were not well suited for self-defense. This was a vulnerable place, subject to external powers. While the coves bristled with the export of grasses and livestock in peacetime, during conflicts they were harassed by revenue ships policing the waters and exacting royal taxes.[40]

THE BURNING OF JAMESTOWN

On December 10, 1775, the Reverend Ezra Stiles, minister of the First Baptist Church in Newport, librarian of Redwood Library, and later president of Yale University, wrote in his diary, "This morning we were awakened with the conflagration of Jamestown on Conanicut. An awful sight. The bomb brigg and several Tenders full of marines went over last night, and about v o'clock or a little before day ended and set fire to the Houses. The men continued ravaging and burning till about Noon... ."[41] On the following day, the British returned, according to Stiles:

> *About 1 o'clock yesterday morning a Bomb Brig, 1 schooner, and 2 or 3 armed sloops went to Conanicott and landed upward of Two Hundred marines, Sailors and Negroes at the E. Ferry and marched in three divisions over to the W. Ferry, & set the several houses on fire there, then retreated back set fire to almost every house on each side of the road, & several Houses and*

Barns some distance on the N. & S. side of the Rode, driving out Women & Children, etc… .The Alarm spread, & I am told there are this day Three hundred Men on Conanicutt & Eight hundred upon the Island. The Town in great Consternation.

Houses Burnt & Lost
Widow Hull 1 house
Jos. Clarke, Esq 2 houses & 1 Barn
Thos. Fowler 1 house & 1 Crib
Ben Ellery 2 houses & 1 Store
Benj. Remington 2 houses
Jno. Gardiner 2 houses & 1 Tanyard
Gov. Hutchinson 1 house
Wm. Franklin 2 houses
Abel Franklin 1 house
Bend. Robinson 1 house.[42]

With over fifteen houses destroyed, many residents fled the island. The population decreased from 556 in 1775 to 323 in the following year.[43] At the outbreak of revolution in 1776, a British fleet of frigates filled the East Passage and nearby Newport Harbor and troops occupied Jamestown, remaining until 1779. Recording the features of Narragansett Bay in his topographical chart dated July 22, 1777, the cartographer Charles Blaskowitz noted the wealth of supplies in the region, "The Horses … are strong, the Meat Cattle and Sheep are much the largest in America, the Butter and Cheese excellent, and every necessary of Life in Abundance."[44] The agricultural produce of Conanicut and its position in the East and West Passages made it a valued prize. Blaskowitz further emphasized the critical function of the smaller islands in the bay by his detailed attention to them: "with all the Isles contained therein, among which Rhode Island and Connonicut have been particularly Surveyed, Shewing the true position & bearings of the Banks, Shoals, Rocks & c. as likewise the Soundings: To which have been added the several Works & Batteries raised by the Americans. Taken by Order of the Principal Farmers on Rhode Island."[45] These isolated rocky points, the realm of those few raising livestock and fishing in bountiful waters, had become weapons of war by far-away empires.

At the height of hostilities in 1777, Frederick Mackenzie, a British army officer, also wrote in his diary of the significance of Conanicut and the smaller islands affecting the approaches to Newport and Narragansett Bay:

If the Rebels have any intention of making a serious attack on this Island (Island of Rhode Island), it is probable they will previously endeavor to possess themselves of Cononicut and Prudence, which would facilitate their attempt. We should use every means in our power to keep possession of Cononicut, to prevent the Rebels from fortifying themselves there, and erecting batteries to obstruct the entrance to the harbour, by which we should be much distressed , and our supplies and subsistence rendered extremely precarious, as the Island affords no other harbour, or good landing place but Newport. Batteries on the Dumplings, a part of Cononicut which forms the entrance of the harbour, would greatly annoy vessels from coming.[46]

28. *Attack on Rhode Island, August, 1778.* Map, 1778. Library of Congress. The strategic position of Conanicut is illustrated in this map, as is the exposed nature of the island. Surrounded by ships attempting to dominate the entrance to Narragansett Bay, the island experienced English, American and French troops in its adjacent waters and on its land throughout most of the war.

Among the "rebels," as described by Mackenzie, the Rhode Island Military Census of April 18, 1777 listed John Eldred, Jr., Peleg Eldred, Samuel Carr, Benjamin Carr, Edward Carr, Daniel Weeden, and Joseph Greene among the thirty-two men from the ages of sixteen to fifty from Jamestown who were able to bear arms.[47] Daniel Weeden's father, Daniel Esq., stood firm in his resolve to resist the British:

> *During the Revolutionary War, he [Daniel Weeden, Esq.] was much annoyed by the British troops quartered near the farm on the island. Though a very old man then ... and wholly unable to do any active service for his country ... and when urged to leave his home and seek a less exposed place to live, he said with some energetic expressions—no—they might shoot him on his own doorsteps, as they did his cattle before his eyes, but he would never leave his house to please the British or their allies the Tories whom he heartily despised—and knew some of his old neighbors to be.*[48]

No battles took place on Conanicut, but occupation entailed continued plunder. The British stationed Hessian mercenaries in the town center, reinforced the rocky outcropping of the Dumplings at the narrowest passage between Conanicut and Newport as an artillery battery to guard the East Passage, and created earthwork redoubts at Fox Hill and at Beavertail Point on the very southernmost tip of the island. Locations throughout the island functioned as observation points for approaching ships and the key to successful military control of the entire Narragansett Bay basin. While Newport held the position of the powerful mercantile city, occupied by the British, boasting fine public buildings and wealthy merchants, Jamestown remained a rural enclave, but in war it took on an importance of epic proportions as a gateway to the region. Rich in resources, strategic in its location, Conanicut proved too valuable to be left intact. The burning of Jamestown made the island a desolate, depopulated zone, a hostage to fortune subject to the vagaries of passing armies and navies.

French ships entered Narragansett Bay in 1778 under the command of Jean Baptiste Charles Henri Hector, Comte d'Estaing, a name as long as his august lineage as a member of an ancient noble family (Fig. 28). His ships successfully drew the British fleet away from the coast to engage in battle, depriving the British army in Newport of supplies, but a storm scattered the ships and d'Estaing moved his vessels on to the West Indies. Only with the retreat of the British and the arrival of the French fleet under the command of Admiral de Ternay and troops under the Comte de Rochambeau

in 1780 did the situation dramatically alter. Mythic heroes entered the scene. On August 19, 1780, the Town Council meeting voted on a resolution to form a committee to "Prepare and Address to their Excellencies the Count de Rochambeau and the Chevalier de Ternay commander of his most Christian fleet in the harbour of Newport. Praying that the people under his command might not be Permitted to come on shore without some Good and Known officer over them in order to Restrain them from Committing Damage or offering injury or insult to the Good and Peaceable People of this town."[49] The French reinforced the batteries, stationed artillery on the redoubts, and awaited the arrival of General Washington, who transited across Conanicut en route to meet Rochambeau and de Ternay on the ship *Duc de Burgoyne* in March of 1781.[50]

With the end of the war and independence for the newly created United States of America, Jamestown lay largely in ruins, its population depleted. This situation is made clear in its citizens' petition to the Rhode Island General Assembly for tax relief, revealing the degree of property loss:

> *It is well known that not one town in the union has suffered so much as Jamestown during the war, more than half of the dwelling houses together with all the out houses, fences wood, stock household furniture be destroyed by the enemy, we have no property in the town to tax but the land only and that reduced in its general quality one third, but to convince your Honours and the world that we are willing to pay a full proportion for what we have left, as New Shoreham and Jamestown hard near alike before the war are willing to take the same proportion as they have in the present tax.*[51]

Jamestown had only the sea and soil after years of war and occupation. Meadows and stone walls remained, and, in time, sheep and other livestock returned as the foundation of the economy. Peace returned, pastoral life continued.

YEARS OF PASTORAL PEACE: 1783–1873

In the wake of the War for Independence, Conanicut Island quietly moved with the years, mostly unnoticed by the rest of the world for almost a century. Known for the quality of its livestock and the hay from its fields, the island remained a remote place, connected only with the mainland by sailing vessels plying the waters of Narragansett Bay. The arduous task of reestablishing buildings and lands damaged or destroyed during the war took time and toil. The Society of Friends built a new meeting house in 1786, and Baptist and Episcopal houses of worship were constructed to support those small congregations. Many of the descendants of the original proprietors, such as the Carrs, the Watsons, the Howlands, and the Weedens, worked to revitalize their holdings (Fig. 29).

By the early 1780s, the Weeden family had reestablished their farms. Daniel Weeden, Esq. divided his extensive lands between his sons, John and Daniel, Jr.; John's homestead numbered 258 acres with five dwellings, two horses, six oxen, seventeen horned cattle, and two swine. Daniel Weeden, Jr. held 287 acres with five dwellings, two horses, five oxen, nineteen horned cattle, and two swine.[52] Although among the major landholders on the island, the Weedens still had to adapt to substantial changes in the way agricultural life and labor were pursued on the island in the post-war era. In 1784, the General Assembly of Rhode Island enacted the Gradual Abolition Act following a lengthy campaign initiated by the Society of Friends to abolish slavery. It stated,

> *Whereas all Men are entitled to Life, Liberty and the Pursuit of Happiness, and the holding of Mankind in a state of Slavery as Private Property, which has gradually obtained by unrestrained Custom and the Permission of the Laws, is repugnant to the Principle, and subversive to the Happiness of Mankind, the great end of All Civil Government. Be it therefore enacted.*

Four months prior to this act, Daniel Weeden, Esq. had manumitted the enslaved on his lands in his will as follows:

> *I give unto my three Negro men named Ben, Tom, and Toby and my Negro woman named Betty their freedom at my decease ... but if either or all of my Negroes shall refuse to take their freedom my mind and will is that he, she or they to refusing shall be taken care of and supported by my executors hereafter named... . On order my executors manumit and set free my two Negro boys called York and London when they shall arrive respectively to the age of twenty three years and my mind and will is that they faithfully serve my son John Weeden till they respectively reach that age.*[53]

29. Carl Ernst Bohn. *Rhode Island* (detail). Map, 1797. Library of Congress.

Greenwich
North
Wickford
Kingstown
South
Kingstown
Tower Hill
Judith Spitze
Potowome
Hunts Fl.
Maskechusick Spitze
NARRAGANSET
Patience
Hog Island
Arnolds Sp.
Calf Pasture Sp.
Despair I.
Hope Island
Prudence
zu Portsmouth
Sandy Pt.
Coggeshall Sp.
Seconiquonset Spitze
Dyke I.
Portsmouth
Black Rock
Connonicut Sp.
BAY
Updykes Harbour
White Rock
Pinders Sp.
Cold Spring Rock (Klippe)
Plumb-beach Sp.
Half-way Rock
Duck Cove
Fox Island
Cranstons Cove
Gould I.
Weavers Cove
RHODE ISLAND
Bifsel's Hill
Coles Harbour
Coles Ledge and Sp.
Coddington's Sp.
Middletown
Bishops Rock
Coaster Harbour
North Fähre
Fahrt
Blue Rock
Taylors Sp.
Rose I.
West Fähre
Dutch I.
NEWPORT
Goat I.
South Fähre
Beaver Head
Bumpling Rocks
Brentons Cove
Pond
the Bonnet
Narraganset Fahrt
Rhode Island Hafen
Newport
the Whale
Beaver's Tail
Brentons Landspitze und Rif
Seal Rock (Klippe)
Price's Neck
Coggeshall's Ledge
Gull Rock
Eastons Bay
Eastons Sp.
Sachueast Bay
Shooling Rock
Robert Lawton
Sachueast Sp.
Flint Rock (Klippe)
Islands Rocks (Klippe)
Cormorant Rock
Seakonnet Fahrt
Common Fence Sp.
Gould I.
Black Sp.
Sandy Sp.
Fogland Fähre
Little Sandy Sp.
Black Sp.
Brown's Sp.
Church's Sp.
Woods Castle
Little Cr.
Easton
Whitehall
Fulling M.
Howland Fähre
OCEAN
RHODE ISLA

Abolition allowed for the freedom of the enslaved, but they faced dire economic circumstances. Without property, they could not move to other communities, where public officials known as "Overseers of the Poor" monitored their activities and often ordered their removal from towns. In 1819, Freelove Howland, a child of parents enslaved by the Howland and Weeden families, and her daughter Betsy were brought before the Newport Town Council for illegal residence. Their story is one of continual bondage, whether named enslavement or indenture, as the Town Council ruled,

> *who saith that she was born on Jamestown and was bound out to James Gould of this town where she lived until she was seventeen years of Age, that her father was named Quam Howland, slave to Isaac Howland and her mother was Violet Weeden of Jamestown aforesaid. That she the said Freelove was never Married, but that she has got one Child, a girl of about Two Months Old... . Wherefore it is ordered that the said Freelove and her Child be removed to Jamestown by and Order of Removal.*[54]

Once removed to Jamestown, Freelove and Betsy were assigned to Benjamin Chapill, who was reimbursed by the town for expenses for their maintenance.[55] Thus, many of the emancipated in Jamestown remained in the employ of their former enslavers, indentured to others as the price of their financial destitution, or served as low-paid laborers. As an agriculturally based economy, Conanicut offered little cash for its laborers and less opportunity for advancement. Toby and York Weeden, formerly enslaved by Daniel Weeden, Esq. and serving his son John after their manumission, were listed in the 1790 census as the heads of households with Toby's numbered at eight other free persons and York's at four free persons.[56] While they may have been listed as free, there is no indication of the accumulation of personal property. The African, African Americans, and Native Americans brought to or born in Jamestown were tied to the land through direct legal means or through economic circumstance.

The case of Job Watson presents a different view of an individual's rise in Jamestown due to the factors of race, gender, and the freedom to pursue one's activities unburdened by restrictive laws. Arriving in the eighteenth century, the town almost denied permission for the penurious Job to settle on the island. In fact, by 1784, he owned 360 acres of land, thirty-three cows, four oxen, one two-year-old heifer, twelve hogs, seven silver spoons, six silver teaspoons, cash 5d.[57] By 1796, Watson was listed as the town's largest landowner.[58] His descendants would also play a major role in real estate development during the nineteenth century as Conanicut evolved into a summer resort.

The land continued to be Conanicut's main asset during the course of the nineteenth century. By 1850, 5,500 acres were devoted to agriculture, with forty-five farms accounting for ninety-three percent of the value of the town: over half used for pasture and hay and only fifteen percent plowed and devoted to crops. The population of approximately four hundred people was accompanied by 1,444 sheep.[59] To these were added cows, lambs, and pigs. In essence, the island supplied livestock for slaughter and cheese and milk. During the Civil War, the Federal government fortified Dutch Island, again seeing the strategic significance of the region. No Confederate invasion disturbed the peace of Jamestown's landscape, which continued its agricultural cycle through the seasons.

One of the most significant events on the island, both in real and symbolic terms, was the reconstruction of the windmill. Conanicut had no sources for water power, only the wind. The earlier colonial era mill had fallen into disrepair. Located on the farm of Joseph Wanton, a loyalist, who had fled Rhode Island in 1779, the state confiscated his property and, in 1787, the General Assembly granted half an acre of the farm to Jamestown for the mill.[60] Operating from the 1780s until 1876, the mill functioned during the years of Conanicut's rebuilding until the advent of a new phase in the life of the island, a picturesque summer retreat. This same mill, an emblem of the functioning agricultural life of the island since colonial settlement, became a historical artifact during the years it lay dormant, an architectural reminder of a long-ago time viewed through a romantic lens.

While the inhabitants of Conanicut farmed and fished, those on the mainland pursued a very different type of activity: industrialization. The northern areas of Rhode Island, namely Providence and the Blackstone River Valley, became leading centers of technological innovation and industrial growth. The southern coast of Rhode Island, comprising Newport on Aquidneck Island, Conanicut, and Narragansett, appeared as sleepy backwaters, their vibrant colonial past a marker of historical memory. However, the romanticism embraced by nineteenth-century art, literature, and culture combined with industrial technology provided the engines of change to coastal Rhode Island. After almost a century of pastoral peace, one of primarily subsistence farming, a period of prosperity based on its picturesque appeal and the power of newly invented steamships would change the course of history, the land, and buildings on Conanicut.

R 78.

4 PICTURESQUE RETREAT: THE RESORT ERA

"... varied avenues and drives affording delightful and picturesque views of islands, channels, the ocean, and the hills of the mainland. This place is designed for private residence—summer homes—and not for public parades, the flaunts of fashion, and the confusion of excursion parties; it is a charming place for quiet and genteel family residences; the Elysium along the shore."

Reverend Frederick Dennison,
Narragansett Sea and Shore, 1880

Previous pages: William Trost Richards. *Our Afternoon on Conanicut*. Watercolor on paper, 1878. Courtesy of the Pennsylvania Academy of the Fine Arts. Gift of Dorrance H. Hamilton in memory of Samuel M. V. Hamilton.

THE APPEAL OF PICTURESQUE SCENERY AND the efficiency of steamship and rail combined to make Conanicut flourish as a summer resort, beginning in the 1870s. While the wealth of the burgeoning Industrial Revolution produced advanced technologies, the taste of many turned away from such modernity when seeking a seasonal escape. Nature reigned supreme. The rocks, coves, coastline, and meadowlands of Conanicut, for centuries accessible by sail, could now be more easily reached via steam (Figs. 30 and 31). One could have one's comforts and partake of a rustic retreat full of picture-perfect views. William Trost Richards, leading painter of the luminist movement in the mid-nineteenth century, was the artist to make the perfect picture and fully explore the picturesque beauties of Conanicut (Fig. 32). With him came the urbanites seeking a peaceful summer refuge in a genteel form, accessible but just removed enough from the noise, bustle, and fashionable foibles of the mainland. Then, the real estate developers, hoteliers, architects, and urban planners began to shape the land and its buildings. The result was a flurry of construction activity from the 1870s through the 1920s, producing an architecture that can without exaggeration be labeled as whimsical, with forms and materials responding to and embedded in its landscape setting. Observers of the early resort extolled its potential:

30. *Ladies Painting*. Photo, ca. 1895. Jamestown Historical Society.

There are a thousand home sites, as cheap as they are desirable, waiting for tenants, though situated in one of the most salubrious climates in the world. I do not know any place where as great a result may be obtained by a little intelligent and scientific foresting as upon the islands of Narragansett Bay. Nature seems to have planned here a great sanitarium, where the clean breezes of the ocean, tempered by the great heat storage of the bay, promise immunity from half the ills to which human flesh is heir.[61]

31. *Jamestown Waterfront*. Photo, ca. 1900. Jamestown Historical Society.

There lies, near the mouth of beautiful Narragansett Bay a pleasant island. ... Parallel with the island of Rhode Island, and not more than two miles distant from it, it is even nearer to the mainland on the other side, here called the Narragansett country. Nine miles in length and with some diversity of high and low lands, Conanicut affords a variety of delightful views, and has preserved, to a remarkable extent, its country like appearance, in spite of its close proximity to so fashionable a summer resort as Newport.

Maud Lyman Stevens, *The Jamestown Windmill*, 1916

The southern portion of Narragansett Bay, its islands, shoreline and historic seaside towns, experienced a major transformation in the mid-nineteenth century as their scenery and climate attracted summer visitors (Figs. 33–41). During the colonial period, most of these coastal communities prospered with maritime trade, their access to the sea a major benefit. However, with the emergence of railroads, which ran on the mainland from New York to Providence to the north and on to Boston, the coastal towns and assorted islands became isolated outposts.

Large-scale factories linked to rail prospered in the northern mainland of Rhode Island, while the southern coastal region remained primarily devoted to agriculture and fishing. Entrepreneurs realized that the cool ocean breezes did have potential for a new enterprise: the resort. An entire industry of steamships offered access to these places, which were marketed to an ever-widening audience. Most noticeable in the burgeoning literature on Narragansett Bay is the constant use of the word "picturesque."

32. William Trost Richards. *Jamestown, Conanicut Island, near Newport*. 1878. Watercolor and Chinese white on paper. Courtesy of the Pennsylvania Academy of the Fine Arts. Gift of Dorrance H. Hamilton in memory of Samuel M. V. Hamilton.

33. *Canonicus Avenue*. Photo, ca. 1895. Jamestown Historical Society. Canonicus Avenue displays the evolving nature of Jamestown in the 1890s, with a chandler's boathouse in the foreground, but none of the other remnants of the colonial town any longer evident. Bathhouses, the Bayview Hotel, and the Thorndike Hotel (background) catered to summer visitors arriving at the nearby ferry landing.

34. *Gardner House and Bayview Hotel*. Postcard, ca. 1900. Jamestown Historical Society.

35. *Workers Building the Bayview Hotel*. Photo, 1889. Jamestown Historical Society.

36. *Bayview Hotel*. Photo, ca. 1900. Jamestown Historical Society.

BAYVIEW HOUSE.

37. *Steamboat Landing*. Photo, ca. 1900. Jamestown Historical Society. The east ferry landing pier is in the foreground, while the Conanicut Park Hotel rises on the hill. Nearby Conanicut Park, the brainchild of Lucius Davis, was the first resort development established in 1873, the same period as the arrival of the first steam-powered ferries.

38. *The Moorings*. Photo, ca. 1890. Jamestown Historical Society. The enterprising Captain Steven Gardner, a ferryboat captain and later proprietor of the nearby eponymous Gardner Hotel, built his Victorian cottage in 1887.

39. *Union Cottage*. Photo, ca. 1890. Merrill Smith Collection. Jamestown Historical Society. The decorative carvings along the roof gable, known as "bargeboards," were typical of picturesque cottages in the period 1840–80. A new aesthetic in the Jamestown cottage would appear in the 1880s with the bold forms and unadorned surfaces of the Shingle Style house of Charles L. Bevins.

40. *Ladies on Porch of Gardner House*. Photo, 1889. Rosengarten Album. Jamestown Historical Society.

41. William Gilder. *Dog Cart on Narragansett Avenue*. Photo, ca. 1900. Jamestown Historical Society.

42. *West Ferry*. Photo, ca. 1920. Jamestown Historical Society.

43. William Gilder. *East Ferry*. Photo, 1891. Jamestown Historical Society.

Writers produced pamphlets and booklets on Narragansett Bay and its resorts with commentary on the character of each locale, its scenery, types of accommodation and visitor amenities, and access by steamship (Figs. 42 and 43). Among the notable works are *Picturesque Narragansett* by Robert Grieve and *Pleasant Places in Rhode Island, and How to Reach Them* (1893) by Mariana M. Tallman. The title of Edwin Mayhew Bacon's booklet—*Narragansett Bay: Its Historic and Romantic Associations and Picturesque Setting* (1904)—encapsulates the key features of Conanicut's appeal. The stage was set, its picturesque backdrop in place, its promoters spreading the word in pen and in photos to build an audience, and its cast of characters in readiness for the play to unfold.

THE CHARACTER OF THE PLACE AND ITS CAST OF CHARACTERS

> *"Conanicut Park is emphatically a place of rest; its diversions, though many, are of the mildest, its dissipations none."*
>
> Mariana M. Tallman, *Pleasant Places in Rhode Island, and How to Reach Them*, 1893

THE FIELDS, STONE WALLS, AND HAYSTACKS of rural life, and the cliffs, cottages, and hotels of resort pastimes defined the character of Conanicut in the nineteenth and early twentieth centuries, a place noted for scenic beauty, a healthy seaside climate, and a tranquil social atmosphere. Agriculture remained prominent on Conanicut, but many farms also became the canvas for new summer communities. Conanicut Park (1872), facing the East Passage at the northern end of the island, Ocean Highlands (1875), to the south on the old Cottrell farm, and Shoreby Hills (1896), adjacent to the village of Jamestown, are three areas platted out by developers with access to ferry landings (Figs. 44–52). Individuals also commissioned cottages along the eastern and southern cliffs, creating a series of Queen Anne and Shingle Style buildings with inventive compositions of roof gables, dormers, towers, and expansive porches that seemingly emerge from rock outcroppings and meadows and then submerge back into them.

Lucius Davis envisioned Conanicut Park in 1872. A resident of Newport, editor of *Gardens and Gardening*, publisher of the *Newport Daily News*, and a member of Newport's Town and Country Club, counting among its members the poet Julia Ward Howe and architect Richard Morris Hunt, Davis had connections and clout.[62] With the first steamship line to Conanicut established in 1873, all was ripe for action. As a former Methodist minister, Davis looked to Wesleyan Grove, the Methodist summer camp on Martha's Vineyard, as a model. He enlisted Henry Lippitt, governor of Rhode Island, as president of the

44. *Swimming*. Photo, ca. 1915.
Meredith and Clarke Album.
Jamestown Historical Society.

45. *Seaside Cottage, Conanicut Park*. Postcard, 1911. Sue Maden Postcard Collection. Jamestown Historical Society.

corporation for the park, with financial backing from Newport summer colonists and Providence textile magnates. As developer of the recently completed Cliff Cottage Association in Newport, Davis had the skill set to launch Conanicut Park. With the purchase of five hundred acres on the northeastern side of the island, he engaged the topographical engineer and surveyor John Mullin to lay out the property in 1873.[63] In April of 1873, cottage lots went on sale. Deeds stipulated that a cottage of a style approved by the company be built within a year, with appropriate landscaping. A highly regulated program designed to create a picture-perfect retreat, penalties applied

46. John Mullin. *Plan of Conanicut Park*, 1873. Courtesy of the Newport Historical Society.

CONANICUT PARK,
RHODE ISLAND.
FOR PLANS, TERMS, &c.
ADDRESS L.D.DAVIS, Agent.
NEWPORT, R.I.
DRAWN BY JOHN H. MULLIN,
Topographical Engineer,
NEWPORT, R.I.
MARCH, 1873.
Scale, 225 feet to an Inch.
NARRAGANSETT BAY.
The dotted lines are curves of equal elevation showing every 10 feet difference of level above High-water.
BAY VIEW DRIVE
WOODLAWN PARK
THE COMMONS
COUNTY ROAD
CONANICUT AVENUE
HIGHLAND AVENUE
SUMMIT AVENUE
PROSPECT AVENUE
ORCHARD AVENUE
ORCHARD GROVE
UNION AVENUE
ISLAND PARK
CONANICUT MEADOW
LINCOLN STREET
PARK STREET
BROADWAY
HOPKINS STREET
ORIENT AVENUE
BROAD STREET
COMMERCIAL STR
MIDDLE STREET
FAIRVIEW STREET
FRANKLIN PLACE
CIRCUIT AVENUE
SUNNYSIDE AVENUE
SUNNYSIDE PARK
NEWPORT AVENUE
NEW YORK AVENUE
BOSTON AVENUE
PROVIDENCE AVENUE
HILLSIDE AVENUE
VALLEY AVENUE
SPRING STR
Hotel
NARRAGANSETT AVENUE
WARWICK AVENUE
GREEN STREET
ZENETTE STR.
BELLEVUE PL
BEACON PL
ROCK STREET
SENECA STREET
GLENWOOD AVENUE
OCCIDENT AVENUE
WICKFORD AVENUE
TEMPLAR
SUNSET AVENUE
ONYX STREET

47. *Dr. Bates's Maplewood Hotel*. Postcard, ca. 1890. Jamestown Historical Society. The hotel catered to guests seeking healthful sea breezes and a peaceful atmosphere.

48. *Cottage by the Sea, Conanicut*. Postcard, 1939. Jamestown Historical Society.

49. *YMCA, Conanicut Park*. Postcard, 1914. Sue Maden Postcard Collection. Jamestown Historical Society.

to those not in compliance with the provisions of their deed. Thirty lots sold within the first month, and Gothic Revival style wooden cottages lined East Shore Road. Trees bordered thoroughfares, and the Conanicut Hotel rose in 1873. Worth & Brazier, a contracting firm based on Martha's Vineyard, built at least five Conanicut Park cottages.[64] Based on the prospectus and the auspicious beginnings of Conanicut Park, Samuel Drake, in his *Nooks and Corners of the New England Coast* (1875), described it as a retreat "accessible to people who do not keep footmen or carriages, or give champagne breakfasts."[65] Mariana Tallman's aptly named *Pleasant Places in Rhode Island* combined an alluring picture of nature with the appealing image of genteel social gatherings:

> *Its six mile length and one mile width have all the wayside delights of upland and ocean. Wild rose and iris, bayberry and elder-bloom crowd the northern meadow, and by and by a harvest of berries can be had for the gathering.*[66]

The unspoiled landscape, pastoral and nurturing, became the metaphor for virtuous pastimes. Innocents in an innocent paradise appealed to Victorian notions of propriety, and the remote island setting of Jamestown was viewed by Miss Tallman as the ideal haven for young ladies, as she reported:

> *... chaperoned by some not over-severe matron, to take possession of a Conanicut cottage for the summer, and have their fill of innocent and healthy fun. It would be hard to say how many charming girls have learnt proficiency in swimming by a Conanicut season, stimulated by criticism and rivalry, and encouraged by calm waters. Their only complaint is, amid the eulogies of beloved Conanicut, that "you can't spend anything there." Papa has neither to forward occasional checks during the daughter's stay, nor to settle sundry later and appalling bills. Conanicut has no store, no bazaar ... one cannot even buy a stamp there.*[67]

The social whirl and worldliness of nearby Rhode Island resorts, such as Newport to the east and Narragansett Pier to the west, were viewed with mild disapproval or severe disdain, depending upon the commentator. Conanicut's atmosphere was one of repose, relaxation, and privacy, enjoyed in a world apart from the mainland, one which valued the high-minded over high fashion. The sense of purpose, of good deeds, of an air of egalitarianism, pervaded Jamestown. Mariana Tallman extolled these virtues, citing one very special instance of beneficence:

> *But the most notable and praiseworthy feature of the place is the institution known as the "Seaside Cottage," established now for fourteen years by the Providence Fountain Society—the admirable arrangement by which tired, ill, or not overly-wealthy city women and children may have a week or two of change and absolute rest at the small sum of $3 per week. Mrs. Wright, the matron, has charge of the fourth season and her domain is a delightful one. Picture a quaint, gray old fashioned farmhouse with deep well and flat door stones, enlarged by an ell and verandas, and nestled in the heart of a quiet old apple orchard, with huge gnarled trunks where sun and shade frolic in the breezes that blow up from the salt waves lapping at the rocks almost at its foot.*[68]

A place to be free, within the confines of Victorian respectability and the safety of an island: Conanicut provided these opportunities where one could be democratic, but within the social comfort of one's own porch surrounded by like-minded souls (Figs. 53–62). The quiet of Conanicut did not attract the overtly fashionable or the scandalous. Scenic views and fine swimming did not offer enough temptations. Tallman approved of the atmosphere and noted that a "general bustle is in the air; and so is the Philadelphia and St. Louis accent, for these two cities populate the most of this growing summer town."[69] The Mid-Atlantic and Mid-Western contingent of summer visitors appeared

50. *Albert Caswell Residence*. Photo, ca. 1900. Jamestown Historical Society. The wooden bracing on the exterior of this cottage was a Stick Style feature, made popular in nearby Newport. This was a variation on the many picturesque types of houses, such as Gothic Revival, Italianate, and Second Empire French, that appeared in Jamestown in the 1870s and remained popular until being largely displaced by the Shingle Style.

51. *Thorncroft*. Photo, ca. 1890. Jamestown Historical Society. Built in 1860 by Jamestown residents Joseph and Robert Watson.

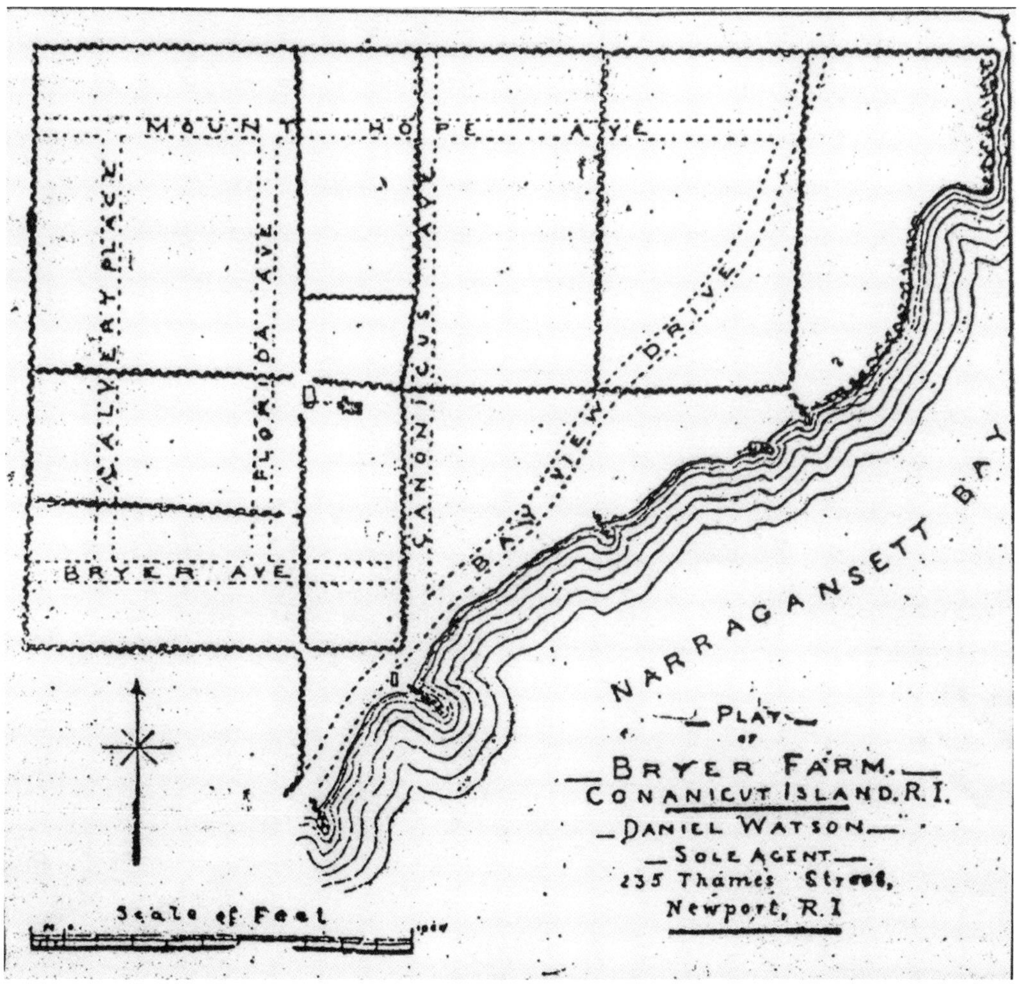

52. *Plat Plan for Subdivision of Bryer Farm* (featured in the *Newport Daily News* of December 13, 1884). Jamestown Historical Society. Daniel Watson, of the family long established as major landowners on Conanicut since the late eighteenth century, based himself in Newport and marketed Jamestown sites with water views for summer house construction. His advertisement focuses on the site's proximity to Newport's amusements while providing the quiet of Conanicut.

53. *Young Ladies and a Maypole.* Photo, August 4, 1928. Jamestown Historical Society.

to prefer the quiet solitude of Conanicut, a place they made their own, where they protected their privacy and shaped their communities to their own liking.

Lucius Davis's dream of Conanicut Park as an Elysian grove diminished somewhat with the economic panic of 1873. Not all house lots were filled, but the Conanicut Hotel emerged as a popular gathering spot, and in the 1880s construction resumed with vigor. Gardner House (1883), the Harbor View Inn (1887), and the Thorndike Hotel (1889) enjoyed sea views from Canonicus Avenue, which served as a popular spot for promenades and gatherings on hotel porches (see Figs. 34 and 115).

Regardless of financial boom and bust, the resort still retained its appeal. However, rather than Conanicut Park, the creation in 1875 of the Ocean Highlands Company, with George C. Carr as president, on over three hundred acres of the Cottrell farm, the rocky outcroppings of "The Dumplings" and nearby cliffs and coves, shifted the focus of resort building to the southern end of the island (see Figs. 79–85). The physical character of the place was picturesque; its social character was intentionally quiet, subject to restrictions by the order of the Ocean Highlands Company as follows:

> *The land is sold with the understanding that no slaughter-house, smith-shop, steam-engine, furnace, forge, bone-boiling establishment, iron or brass foundry, no manufactory of chemicals of any description, of gas, soap, fish guano, fish oil, kerosene or other oil, no brewery, distillery, bar, ale-house, drinking saloon, or other place for the manufacture, compounding or selling of any kind of intoxicating liquors in any manner or form, shall ever be erected, located, used or suffered, in or upon any part of said granted land; and that no other noxious, dangerous or offensive trade or business whatever shall ever be done, carried on, or permitted in or upon said land or any part thereof.*

54. *Eight Golfers Sitting on Bleecker's Box Porch.* Photo, 1896. Bleecker Album. Jamestown Historical Society.

55. *Mr. and Mrs. J. Rosengarten and Sam on the Porch of Their Cottage.* Photo, ca. 1890. Rosengarten Album. Jamestown Historical Society. Curvaceous Italianate brackets adorn the roof of the Rosengarten porch.

56. *Young People on a Pier*. Photo, ca. 1900. Meredith and Clarke Album. Jamestown Historical Society.

57. *Carr Family Sailing and Boating*. Photo, ca. 1900. Jamestown Historical Society.

58. *Children's Lawn Party*. Photo, ca. 1900. Meredith and Clarke Album. Jamestown Historical Society. The Thorndike Hotel is in the background.

59. William Trost Richards. *The Children's Tennis Court, Conanicut Island*. Watercolor and Chinese white on paper, 1883. Courtesy of the Pennsylvania Academy of the Fine Arts. Gift of Dorrance H. Hamilton in memory of Samuel M. V. Hamilton. Richards primarily focused on maritime and meadowland scenes in his work, but here he depicts children at tennis with a dog in the road. However, the human and canine presence is small compared to his rendering of their landscape setting.

60. *Lawn Party at Men's Club*. Photo, ca. 1900. Merrill Smith Collection. Jamestown Historical Society. A small island with an active, albeit sedate, social scene, Conanicut offered boating, swimming, and social clubs to entertain summer residents. The buildings in this photograph date to the 1870s and early 1880s, proper Victorian wooden boxes with restrained wooden ornamentation along rooflines and gables.

61. *Conanicut Yacht Club and Reading Room.* Photo, ca. 1895. Jamestown Historical Society.

62. *Maria A. & A. A. Hirst Jr. with Their Ponies Belle Meade and John – Flower Parade, August 15, 1901.* Photo, 1901. Jamestown Historical Society.

With the exception of the nature-made sounds of wind and waves, the human occupants of Ocean Highlands required their peers to safeguard quiet, a quality so prized it was commented upon in the press, "What is the chief attraction of Jamestown?" we asked an old settler. "Well, it's the climate and the quiet," he answered. "Any number of Westerners come here who object to Newport and the Pier because they are not quiet."[70]

With the sale of the Cottrell farm in 1884, and its subdivision and road systems laid out by 1887, hundreds of acres in the Ocean Highlands district facing the East Passage, the Atlantic Ocean to the south, and Mackerel Cove to the west became available for a building boom. Such activity and the changes it wrought were quick and notable, so much so that the *Providence Journal* reported in 1887, "Green fields have abounded and farmers have thrived throughout its limits, but with the influx of summer residents whole tracts of land have lost their identity as farms, and a new era in history begins."[71] Farming now shared space with summer hotels, cottages, and fishing camps (Figs. 63–69).

Real estate developers worked tirelessly to promote the area, selling lots of land. However, it took an artist to enter the scene, and a brilliant scene-maker indeed, in William Trost Richards, to call out the appeal of the picturesque island through words and pictures. A painter of coastline, meadows, and seascapes in oil and notably in watercolor, Richards declared: "[C]ertainly there is no place more lovely than Conanicut in all the world."[72]

63. *Susan Franklin Cottage*. Photo, ca. 1910. Jamestown Historical Society. Set within the vast fields near Hull Cove, the Franklin cottage was a truly rustic retreat within sight of a roaring ocean, a rich area for fishing, and still retaining the hay fields cultivated for centuries.

64. *Susan Franklin Cottage, Porch View*. Photo, ca. 1910. Jamestown Historical Society.

65. *Grey Ledge Tea Room, Beavertail.* Postcard, 1909. Jamestown Historical Society. The Alexander cottage became a tea room near the Beavertail fishing camp in this remote southern portion of Conanicut.

66. *Eliza Alexander House, Grey Ledge.* Photo, ca. 1920. Jamestown Historical Society. Wilson Eyre, Jr., a Philadelphia architect and founder of *House and Garden* magazine, designed this simplified shingled building marked by a sweeping roofline and expansive arch. Eyre admired the work of fellow Arts and Crafts architects, such as the English designer Charles Annesley Voysey and Sir Edwin Lutyens, whose buildings displayed a similar combination of boldness and streamlined forms.

67. *Robert W. Golet Fishng Camp and Tea House*. Postcard, ca. 1920. Jamestown Historical Society. Beavertail provided the perfect setting for fishing camps. Robert Goelet, who summered in nearby Newport, maintained a fishing camp, and the adjacent Alexander house eventually became a tea house, providing a social outlet in this isolated part of Conanicut.

68. *William Franklin's Fishing Shack*. Photo, ca. 1906. Jamestown Historical Society. William Franklin's fishing shack at Hull Cove was eventually replaced by Susan Franklin's more substantial, yet still decidedly simple, house.

69. *Fishermen, Beavertail Road*. Photo, ca. 1900. Jamestown Historical Society.

WILLIAM TROST RICHARDS: THE PAINTER AND THE PERFECT PICTURE

In watercolor, William Trost Richards created images of land and sea evoking a variety of moods: storm-tossed cliffs, gentle sun-drenched meadows, shadowed green groves. He produced these works at home and abroad: the cliffs of Cornwall, the coast of Newport, and almost every corner of Conanicut Island, visiting in the 1870s and finally building a house, called Grey Cliff (1882), in the Ocean Highlands area, where he lived and painted for the remainder of his life (Fig. 70). In the summers Richards went exploring, "prospecting" as he called it, to observe nature and make drawings, using these as he developed his watercolors. Richards truly adopted Conanicut as his subject just at the point when he emerged as a national figure on the American art scene. His works form an impressive record of the various points on the island, and these same points provided inspiration for his evolving aesthetic and technique.

By the time William Trost Richards settled on Conanicut Island, he had achieved substantial renown as an Honorary Member of the National Academy of Design. His early work focused on the woodlands of the White Mountains in New Hampshire. Born in Philadelphia, Richards became a draftsman and, in the early 1850s, studied and exhibited his work at the Pennsylvania Academy of the Fine Arts. He became associated with an influential group of American painters—the Hudson River School—and the romanticized landscapes of Frederick Church, John Frederick Kensett, Albert Bierstadt, Suzie Barstow, Eliza Pratt Greatorex, and Harriet Cany Peale. The American Pre-Raphaelites' emphasis on landscape and the writings of the English critic John Ruskin,

---

"... the trustees of the Corcoran Gallery have made a strenuous effort to get together ... a good representative showing of American pictures... . Americans who believe in American art, especially American landscape art, have had placed before their eyes pictures of which this nation has reason to be proud. Side by side are pictures by Frederick Church, [Asher] Durand, George Innes, [Worthington] Whittredge ... and [John Frederick] Kensett. Nearby are works by Thomas Cole, W.T. Richards ... all of whom are dear to American hearts."

"Landscape Art of American Painters,"
Washington Post, 1902

70. William Trost Richards. *Salt Works Beach, Conanicut Island*. Watercolor and Chinese white on paper, 1877. Chinese white is an opaque-white watercolor made from zinc-oxide pigment. It was first introduced in the 1830s as a replacement for lead white watercolor, which darkened when exposed to sulfur in the air. Richards often mixed transparent watercolor with the opaque Chinese white or gouache. Courtesy of the Pennsylvania Academy of the Fine Arts. Gift of Dorrance H. Hamilton in memory of Samuel M. V. Hamilton.

specifically *Modern Painters* (1843), and the focus on *plein air* painting all played their part in Richards's evolution as an artist. According to artist Worthington Whittredge, *Modern Painters* was "in every landscape painter's hand."[73] Small exhibition magazines like *The Crayon*, first published by William James Stillman in 1855, popularized the art of the Pre-Raphaelite Brotherhood.[74] Richards knew and exhibited with this circle of artists, particularly Church, Kensett, and Stillman, all of whom made their way to the Rhode Island coast, specifically Newport, from the 1850s through the 1870s. Church and Kensett were founders of the Metropolitan Museum of Art in 1871, and Stillman, renowned for his photographs of the Acropolis in Athens and other ancient sites, also came to Newport in 1872 to record images of colonial buildings for the architect Charles Follen McKim.

While well connected with artistic circles in Philadelphia and New York, and finding fame in these cities, Richards chose Conanicut because of its remoteness. He made the idyllic island the muse for his life's work. In his Conanicut images, he would move away from the idealized landscapes of the Hudson River School and the ethereal quality of Pre-Raphaelite works as he began to explore topographical detail, light, and atmosphere in the medium of watercolor.

WILLIAM TROST RICHARDS AND THE TRIUMPH OF WATERCOLOR

The founding of the American Watercolor Society in New York in 1866 marked a key moment in the advance of the artistic medium. In 1878, the society held its exhibition at the National Academy of Design in New York, with *South-West Point, Conanicut* by William Trost Richards one of the largest works on display. His soft flowing brushwork of the later 1870s has an impressionist quality, and the rough texture of the fibrous paper he used for canvas lent itself ideally to the rendering of rugged cliffs and surging waves. Richards also used gouache, an opaque watercolor mixed with white pigment, that had the richer qualities of oil paint. He also often highlighted details in pen and black ink.

As his art evolved, marine watercolors became his primary subject matter and medium and Conanicut Island served as the perfect setting. From the porch of his house with views in every direction, he accomplished a prolific amount of work. With the medium of watercolor, he captured the fluid quality of haze, oftentimes barely discernible, that descended upon Narragansett Bay depending upon the temperature of the sea and air and the changing nature of the weather. Delicate dabs of pale blue and gray in the sky, rich mixtures of green and touches of red in the land each spoke to the specific qualities of the earth, ocean, and the atmosphere. The result is a luminous series of pictures documenting vantage points from key island locales, and moving beyond mere records of a place to create a timeless landscape, glimmering in changing light and warm earth (Figs. 71–78). As Richards applied watercolor to capture the ephemeral qualities of land, sea, and sky, the writer Thomas Wentworth Higginson, friend and mentor to Emily Dickinson and frequent visitor to nearby Newport, expressed in words the scenes and atmosphere of Narragansett Bay that Richards spent years observing and interpreting on canvas:

71. William Trost Richards. *High Hill, Conanicut Island*. Watercolor on paper, 1877. Courtesy of the Pennsylvania Academy of the Fine Arts. Gift of Dorrance H. Hamilton in memory of Samuel M. V. Hamilton.

72. William Trost Richards. *My Cliffs on Conanicut Island*. Watercolor and Chinese white on paper, 1881. Courtesy of the Pennsylvania Academy of the Fine Arts. Gift of Dorrance H. Hamilton in memory of Samuel M. V. Hamilton.

> *As we looked from the broad piazza, there was a glassy smoothness over all the bay, and the hills were coated with a film, or rather a mere varnish, inconceivably thin, of haze more delicate than any other climate in America can show. Over the water there were white gulls flying, lazy and low; schools of young mackerel displayed their white sides above the surface; and it seemed as if even a butterfly might be seen for miles over that calm expanse. The bay was covered with mackerel-boats, and one man sculled indolently across the foreground a scarlet skiff. It was so still that every white sail-boat rested where its sail was first spread; and though the tide was at half-ebb, the anchored boats swung idly in different ways from their moorings. Yet there was a continuous ripple in the broad sail of some almost motionless schooner, and there was a constant melodious plash along the shore. From the mouth of the bay came up slowly the premonitory line of bluer water, and we knew that a breeze was near.*[75]

Among a group of artists promoting the idea that watercolor could be the equal of oil painting, Richards used large-scale sheets of a fibrous paper, invented as a backing for carpets, in order to give rich texture. Once he applied watercolor and gouache, in vast seascapes, the effect challenged the established canon that oil paintings reigned supreme. The prominent heiress, patron of the arts, and Newport summer resident Catharine Lorillard Wolfe acquired his watercolor *A Rocky Coast* in 1877 for the Metropolitan Museum of Art in New York, of which she was a major benefactor. Like Richards, Miss Wolfe admired the historical, romantic, and picturesque to be found in and around the Narragansett Bay region. In Newport, she lived on Touro Park with its view of an old stone tower, proposed by some to have been built by the Vikings but more likely a seventeenth-century colonial construction. Although not based in documented fact, the monument cast its spell on Miss Wolfe, who, in 1885, built a Romanesque Revival house in red sandstone and a model hen house in wood shingles on Ochre Point, creating an estate with the air of a medieval village perched on cliffs overlooking a vast ocean. The spirit behind Miss Wolfe's Newport estate and Richards's Conanicut watercolors was the same: history, romance, and the picturesque as the foundations for creative expression by artist and patron, whether in stone and wood buildings, on canvas in paintings, or in words in poetry and prose.

73. William Trost Richards. *Entrance to West Cove, Conanicut Island*. Watercolor and Chinese white on paper, 1881. Courtesy of the Pennsylvania Academy of the Fine Arts. Gift of Dorrance H. Hamilton in memory of Samuel M. V. Hamilton.

74. William Trost Richards. *View up the Bay from Conanicut Island*. Watercolor and Chinese white on paper, 1881. Courtesy of the Pennsylvania Academy of the Fine Arts. Gift of Dorrance H. Hamilton in memory of Samuel M. V. Hamilton.

75. Wiliam Trost Richards. *W. T. Richards's House on Conanicut Island.* Watercolor and Chinese white on paper, 1882. Courtesy of the Pennsylvania Academy of the Fine Arts. Gift of Dorrance H. Hamilton in memory of Samuel M. V. Hamilton.

76. Wiliam Trost Richards. *The Road to the House of W. T. Richards, Conanicut Island.* Watercolor and Chinese white on paper, 1882. Courtesy of the Pennsylvania Academy of the Fine Arts. Gift of Dorrance H. Hamilton in memory of Samuel M. V. Hamilton.

77. William Trost Richards. *View from the Front of W. T. Richards's House, Conanicut Island*. Watercolor and Chinese white on paper, 1882. Courtesy of the Pennsylvania Academy of the Fine Arts. Gift of Dorrance H. Hamilton in memory of Samuel M. V. Hamilton.

78. William Trost Richards. *The Road through the Moor, Conanicut Island.* Watercolor and Chinese white on paper, 1882. Courtesy of the Pennsylvania Academy of the Fine Arts. Gift of Dorrance H. Hamilton in memory of Samuel M. V. Hamilton.

PICTURESQUE COTTAGES: THE HOUSE BUILDERS ARRIVE

"The situation + prospect are very fine + certainly the word stable cannot be applied to such a handsome house. ...
Thy ever loving Mother"

Letter from Deborah Fisher Wharton to her son, Joseph, on the progress of his wood shingle and stone house, Horsehead, on the cliffs of Conanicut, 1883

William Trost Richards played a critical role in celebrating the ethereal beauties of Conanicut through his watercolors, while his personal connections made a real impact upon the place, with his fellow Philadephians Joseph and Charles Wharton, the Loverings, Lippincotts, and Clothiers, many interrelated, adopting the eastern and southern coast of the island as their summer enclave in the 1880s (Figs. 79–98), which came to be marked by houses of extraordinary whimsy and individuality. They were followed by a notable collection of naval personnel. At any given time, over thirty admirals, rear admirals, captains, and commanders built summer cottages in Jamestown. The Newport-based architects J. D. Johnston and Charles L. Bevins were largely responsible for the houses commissioned by these patrons. Among this group, the Philadelphia industrialist and financier Joseph Wharton ranked as the wealthiest and most influential.

79. George W. Lake. *View from Fort Dumpling*. Stereoscopic glass plate, 1890. Jamestown Historical Society. The view of Conanicut from Fort Dumpling. The large house is Braecleugh, built 1883. Stornaway and Horsehead are in the background.

80. John Scott Biddle.
Horsehead. Photo, ca. 1950.
Jamestown Historical Society.

81. William Trost Richards. *Boats at Pier for Joseph Wharton's Workmen, Conanicut Island.* Watercolor and Chinese white on paper, 1882. Courtesy of the Pennsylvania Academy of the Fine Arts. Gift of Dorrance H. Hamilton in memory of Samuel M. V. Hamilton.

82. *Ladies on Rocks at Horsehead.* Photo, ca. 1900. Jamestown Historical Society.

83. *The Wharton Family Sailing*. Photo, ca. 1920. Jamestown Historical Society. The Whartons, including Joseph Lovering Wharton, in pith helmet, enjoy the waters of Narragansett Bay in style.

84. *Music on the Lawn of Horsehead*. Photo, ca. 1900. Jamestown Historical Society.

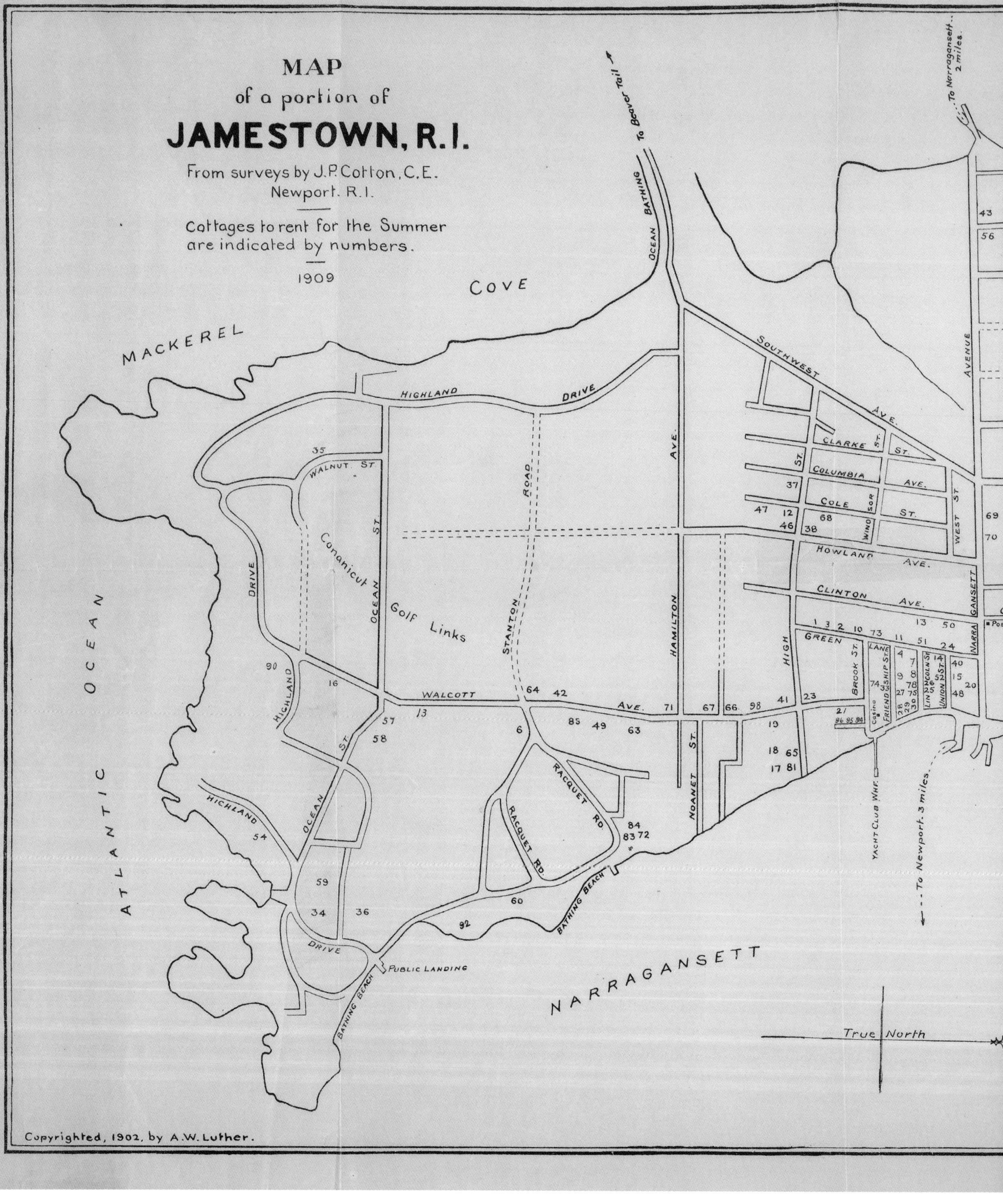
MAP
of a portion of
JAMESTOWN, R.I.
From surveys by J.P. Cotton, C.E.
Newport. R.I.
Cottages to rent for the Summer
are indicated by numbers.
1909
MACKEREL
COVE
ATLANTIC
OCEAN
NARRAGANSETT
To Beaver Tail
To Narragansett... 2 miles.
To Newport. 3 miles.
OCEAN BATHING
HIGHLAND DRIVE
SOUTHWEST AVE.
WALNUT ST.
OCEAN ST.
Conanicut Golf Links
STANTON ROAD
HAMILTON AVE.
CLARKE ST.
COLUMBIA AVE.
COLE ST.
WINDSOR
HOWLAND AVE.
CLINTON AVE.
WEST ST.
NARRAGANSETT AVENUE
GREEN
HIGH ST.
BROOK ST.
LANE
FRIENDSHIP ST.
LINCOLN ST.
UNION ST.
WALCOTT AVE.
NOANET ST.
RACQUET RD.
BATHING BEACH
PUBLIC LANDING
YACHT CLUB WHF.
Casino
Post
True North
Copyrighted, 1902, by A.W. Luther.

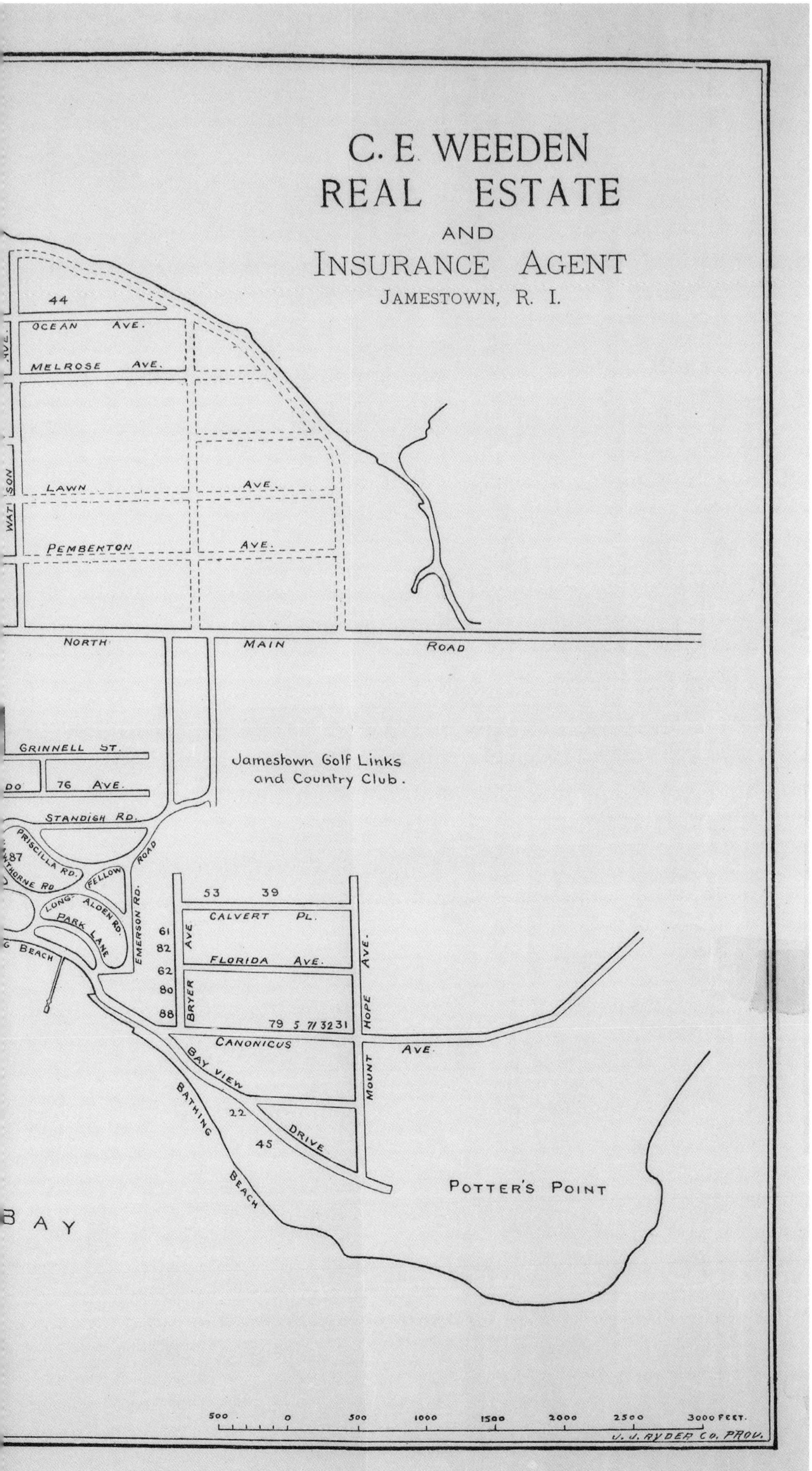

85. *Map of a Portion of Jamestown*, 1908. C. E. Weeden Real Estate and Insurance Agent. Jamestown Historical Society. The map illustrates the development of the resort from Ocean Highlands (lower left) to the center of Jamestown village and the site of the Shoreby Hills area (curved and gridded roads on the right). The Weeden family were among the original settlers of Jamestown, and, like the Carr and Watson families, were instrumental in converting farm holdings into sites for summer houses.

JOSEPH WHARTON: AN INDUSTRIAL TITAN RESHAPES A PICTURESQUE ISLAND

> *"I have known him to ride post-haste from Jamestown, R. I., to Professor Agassiz's distant house in Newport with an uncommon species of marine life for investigation, and his interest in the land crabs of Cuba and the minor animals of the West was great; but his mind ran rather to the larger cosmic sciences, because it was of large mould, and was used to push ahead into speculative paths."*
>
> Harrison S. Morris on Joseph Wharton, *Proceedings of the American Philosophical Society*, 1909

A leading figure in American industry and philanthropy during the Gilded Age, Joseph Wharton (March 3, 1826 – January 11, 1909) literally reshaped the character of the southern sector of Conanicut Island into his picturesque retreat. As a Quaker with two grandmothers, both named Hannah, from Newport, Rhode Island, he originally opted to summer in the Point section of Newport, a district bequeathed to and laid out by the Society of Friends in the early 1700s. When not sailing and exploring the waters of Narragansett Bay, Wharton became an expert in the metallurgy industry, creating the American Nickel Works, investing in mines in western Pennsylvania, and as a major stockholder in the Bethlehem Iron Company, producing pig iron and steel rails. With contracts for the U.S. military and industrial giants, the company grew into Bethlehem Steel and Wharton into one of the titans of American industry. In 1901, a consortium organized by J. P. Morgan purchased Bethlehem Steel and created U.S. Steel, the largest corporation in the world. Fascinated by invention and innovation, Wharton was a colleague to several leading figures in technological advancements: Thomas Edison with developments in electricity, sound, and cinema; Ezra Cornell, a co-founder of Cornell University and an innovator in telegraph along with Samuel Morse; and Elias Howe, the creator of the lockstitch sewing machine. As president of the American Iron and Steel Institute, Wharton served as a major power broker in the national economy. On a personal level, he was a close associate of railroad magnate Cornelius Vanderbilt, steel baron Andrew Carnegie, and was a friend and offered counsel to Presidents Ulysses S. Grant, Rutherford B. Hayes, and Benjamin Harrison.[76] Wharton also engaged in several philanthropic activities, with a focus on education. Along with his mother and fellow Quakers, he founded Swarthmore College in Pennsylvania in 1869. Keenly aware of the monumental shifts in industry, technology, and the systems needed to function in a world economy, he founded the Wharton School of Finance and Economy, now known as the Wharton School, in 1881 at the University of Pennsylvania.[77]

When not directing the life of a vast industrial realm, Wharton retreated to the waters of Narragansett Bay, far from the technological advances and modern factories that had made his fortune. His love of sailing and his acquaintance with William

Trost Richards led him to the pastoral retreat of Conanicut, an island still immersed in the agriculture of earlier centuries. Time seemed to stand still in this remote place, which appealed to Wharton. In 1882, he purchased thirty acres from Ocean Highlands adjacent to Richards's house, Grey Cliff. Enjoying expansive vistas of Newport to the east, open ocean to the south, and Mackerel Cove to the west, Wharton engaged Charles Bevins to design Horsehead on this scenic spot. The massive dwelling rose on the rocks, its oversized tower with a bell-capped roof and stone facade incorporating an open porch framed by heavy Romanesque-style arches lending this house a castle-like air, a monument looming over island and sea. Each facade is marked by a distinctive composition of gabled rooflines, but unified overall by the use of diamond-paned windows and wood-shingled surfaces (Figs. 80–84 and 86). Joseph's mother, Deborah Fisher Wharton, visited the site with her son Charles during construction and shared her thoughts in a letter of July 22, 1883:

My dear son Joseph,
I want thee to know that I took an excursion to Conanicut on the Jamestown steamer, thy brother Charles my escort, Wm + my carriage going on the boat with his. I wanted especially to see thy house + so drove directly there. The exterior far surpassed my expectations + I think when finished it will be very handsome. It was full of divers mechanics busy at their various handicrafts, some finishing the roof. I wanted very much to see the interior, but thy brother thought it would be an improper undertaking for me, in its present condition. Charles however did go in + went all over it, + it surpassed his expectations as well as my own. He may have written to tell thee of our visit, + said he believed if thee + thy family were to come on to Newport, it would forward its completion, + it need not be very long before it was finished. There is no small amount of work yet to be done, but the men seem to be working in good earnest.

Thy ever loving Mother[78]

86. *Aerial View of Horsehead.* Photo, ca. 1950. Jamestown Historical Society.

Wharton's family and fellow Philadephians soon followed his example in the Ocean Highlands and Walcott Avenue districts. Among the cliffs and coves rose Charles Wharton's Braecleugh (1883), Benjamin Shoemaker's Stornaway (1883), the artist James B. Sword's cottage (1883), Dr. R. Griffith's Eglesfeld (1887), Isaac Clothier's Harbor Entrance, Daniel S. Newhall's Round House (1888), J. Bertram Lippincott's Meersblick (1893), and Joseph Lovering Wharton's Clingstone (1905). Prominent naval families were also drawn to this coastline: Admiral Thomas O. Selfridge, Jr.'s The Barnacle (1886), Admiral Wells's Longwood (1886), Admiral Dixon Porter's Belvedere (1888), and his son-in-law Lieutenant L. C. Logan's Meadowside (1888), General R. E. Paterson's Channel Bells, later known as The Ramparts (1888), and Professor Charles Larned's The Boulders (1888) (Figs. 87–109). These cottages illustrate the ingenuity and creativity of both clients and architects. Among the many who shaped the island in the 1880s, two figures stand out. Daniel Watson, descended from one of the original colonial era proprietors, became a key figure along with Charles Bevins in defining the character of Conanicut's resort planning and architecture. The *Newport Mercury* hailed their efforts accordingly:

> *Next to the natural attractions and picturesque beauty of this section of Conanicut Island, Mr. Daniel Watson, the real estate agent, has probably been the most prominent factor in causing the wonderful growth of Jamestown and for the beauty and uniformity of its improvements its patrons should be under lasting obligation to the excellent taste and skill of Mr. Charles L. Bevins, the architect from whose plans nearly all the better class cottages have been built.*[79]

87. *Braecleugh*. Photo, ca. 1900. Meredith and Clarke Album. Jamestown Historical Society. Charles Wharton, a Quaker and industrialist from Philadelphia, commissioned this house from Charles L. Bevins. Built in 1883, it is an asymmetrical composition of encompassing porch, dormers, gables, and shingled surfaces set at the very edge of the rocky coastline. The property was condemned in 1905 for the creation of Fort Wetherill.

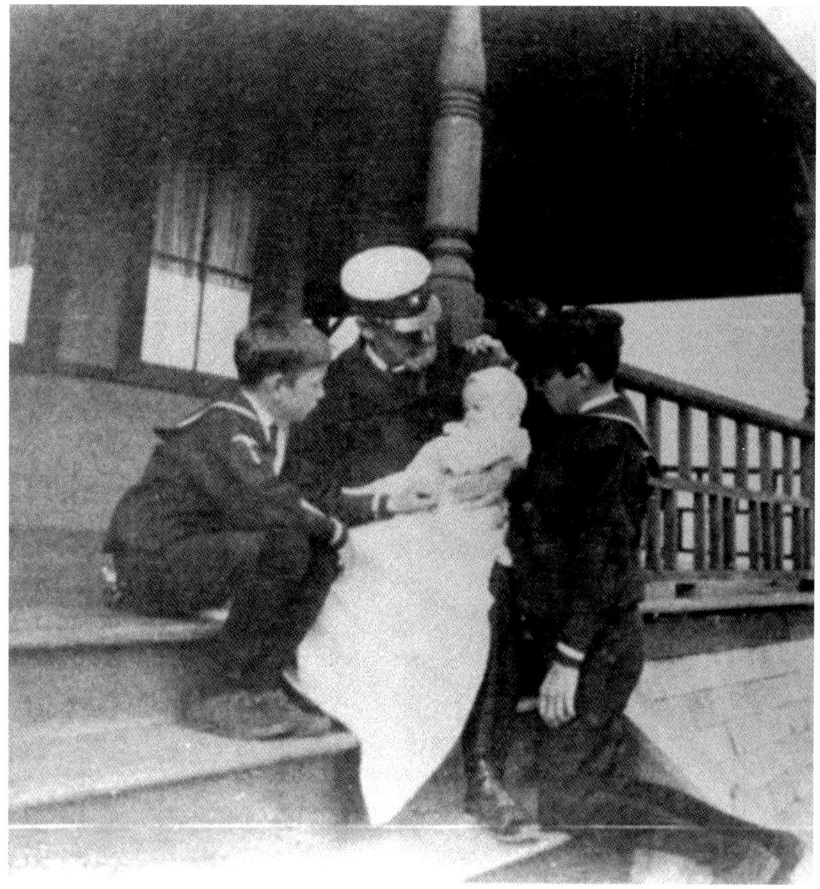

88. *Wharton Family on the Steps of Braecleugh*. Photo, ca. 1900. Jamestown Historical Society. Joseph Samuel Lovering Wharton holding Samuel Brinton Shoemaker Wharton, with Joseph Samuel Lovering Wharton Jr. (left) and Charles William Wharton (right).

89. *View of Braecleugh and Fort Dumpling*. Photo, ca. 1890. Jamestown Historical Society. House and fort, both immersed in their rocky promontories, represent the old and new that formed the appeal of Conanicut in the nineteenth century: the historic associations of the iconic fortification and the innovative design of the C. W. Wharton house, constructed in 1883 during a building boom in resort architecture.

90. *The Ramparts.* Photo, ca. 1900. Jamestown Historical Society. Built for General Robert E. Patterson in 1888 by Charles L. Bevins. A relatively unique approach to massing for Bevins, with an emphasis on the grand scale of the center of the building, faced in latticework inspired by Japanese sources. The house was later referred to as Channel Bells.

92. *Harbor Entrance*. Photo, ca. 1900. Jamestown Historical Society.

91. *Eglesfeld*. Photo, ca. 1900. Meredith and Clarke Album. Jamestown Historical Society. The overarching gambrel roof flows into the walls and porch, uninterrupted by any framing devices, so the house visually blends directly into its rocky hillside. Dr. R. Eglesfeld Griffith commissioned Charles L. Bevins to design this gambrel-roofed cottage in 1886. The windows comprising upper portions of paned glass and lower portions of plate glass are typical of Shingle Style houses of the period. No ornamentation is used on the facade, and the right side of the porch is marked by a curved opening edged in shingles and devoid of any molding. This feature appears often in Bevins buildings and is a device used for the simple and effective framing of views.

93. *Stornaway*. Photo, ca. 1890. Jamestown Historical Society. Built in 1883 for B. H. Shoemaker by Charles L. Bevins with J. D. Johnston as builder. Demolished ca. 1900 for the construction of Fort Wetherill. In this project, Bevins developed a complex roofline with jerkinhead gables (on the right side of the photo) inspired by medieval houses in northern Europe. These angled gables add to the asymmetry of the composition, which complements the asymmetry of the rocky coastal setting. The first-floor windows are of large pieces of plate glass, allowing for generous views and, when opened, ease of movement between interior and exterior.

94. *Joseph Samuel Lovering Wharton (1850–1931) and Amelia Shoemaker Wharton with Their Son Charles Wharton (b. 1893)*. Photo, ca. 1895. Jamestown Historical Society.

95. *Belvedere*. Photo, ca. 1895. Jamestown Historical Society. Built for Admiral Dixon Porter in 1888, this house has a complex series of facades, composed of the extensive porch combining open areas, latticework partially screening some portions, and glass fully protecting other sections. The second floor is marked by small side porches with turned posts, and of particular note are the large-scale curved brackets supporting the roof gable. These are fully shingled and appear in much of Bevins's work. For all of its complexity, the roof is quite simple, offering a sheltering and organizing feature to all of the details below.

96. *Green Chimneys*. Photo, ca. 1900. Meredith and Clarke Album. Jamestown Historical Society. Admiral Thomas O. Selfridge, Jr. engaged Charles L. Bevins to design this house, eventually known as Green Chimneys in 1889, after completion of Selfridge's residence, The Barnacle (1886). Japanese influence is evident in the delicate balustrades and latticework of the two-story porch. While appearing as a basic rectangular form, the house becomes much more complicated as the roof combines a gable on hip at one end and a saltbox profile on the other.

97. *Admiral Wells Cottage*. Photo, ca. 1900. Meredith and Clarke Album. Jamestown Historical Society. Bevins created this picturesque cottage in 1888 for Admiral Wells. The roofline has a jerkinhead gable (left) over a second-floor balcony and terminates in a large-scale gable with a checkerboard grid of decorative openings above windows with transoms of delicate framing inspired by Japanese latticework.

98. *Wells Cottage, Interior*. Photo, ca. 1900. Meredith and Clarke Album. Jamestown Historical Society. Replete with the Victorian fascination for potted palms and generous draping of textiles over doors, the Wells Cottage fireplace is a true Bevins feature: bold, rustic, and in keeping with the spirit of Conanicut.

The collection of cottages, set within a topography of cliff and windswept meadow, is an extraordinarily organic union of architecture and landscape, the critical factor that elevates the significance of this ensemble. Houses are marked by rooflines of sweeping intersecting gables, pronounced window shapes ranging in scale from the diminutive to the oversized in relation to their wall schemes, all-encompassing porches unifying exterior and interior, curvaceous wall brackets, high towers capped by bell-shaped roofs, and the angled projections of wings that prevent any sense of rigid symmetry. Complex architectural compositions are unified by weathered shingled walls winding, with an apparent effortless ease, around corners and curving upwards and downwards along cornices and around balconies. No framing elements interrupt this visual flow of surface material. One notable feature in most buildings is the decided lack of elaborate ornament. There is very little decorative carving or applied stucco, pebble-work, or other materials popular at the time in Queen Anne and Shingle Style design. Instead, the whimsical effect of these houses is achieved through the exaggerated proportions of doors, windows, and dormers, and the asymmetrical massing of square and rectangular forms. These are dwellings of relaxation, informality, and joyousness, reinforced by the playful manipulation of scale, lending a storybook air to these dwellings huddled in waving grass fields and stony outcroppings by the sea.

The Barnacle (1886) is a study in the most dramatic type of siting (Figs. 99–105). Perched atop a rocky promontory, it rises as a series of geometric shapes: squares, rectangles, and triangles, arranged in the most inventive and singular manner, all in the service of creating the most whimsical of dwellings. From a distance, it has the air of a medieval castle with steeply pitched roofs; on closer inspection, each facade plays a different role. Windows dominate on the street-facing elevation featuring the large-scale band of rectangular panes of the interior stairwell. One element that is not prominent is a front door, accessed on the northern side through the shingled arches of the porch. Two sharp gables and the covered porch are the organizing elements on the eastern facade, and the complex cubic forms of the service wing, with kitchens and pantries, form the southern elevation. All of these facades are unified by continuous wood-shingled surfaces rising to a steeply pitched roof. The effect of the whole architectural ensemble is one of a monumental triangle from the base of the rock to the tallest chimney.

Commanding this height was the figure of the owner of The Barnacle, Thomas Oliver Selfridge, Jr., son of a rear admiral and a man with a colorful and controversial naval career. He served in the Civil War, and later, promoted to captain, commanded several ships in the Pacific. While in command of the *Omaha*, he greeted with appropriate fanfare Captain de Saune of the French man-of-war *Isère* upon its arrival in New York harbor on June 18, 1885 to deliver the Statue of Liberty.[80] In 1887, Selfridge was still in charge of the *Omaha*; conducting target practice off the coast of the Japanese island of Ikeshima, he caused the deaths of four Japanese and the wounding of seven others. This created an international incident,

99. *The Barnacle*. Photo, ca. 1900. Jamestown Historical Society. In all of the work of Charles L. Bevins, The Barnacle is the most dramatic in setting and the manner in which the architectural forms are integrated with the natural topography. Built in 1886 for Admiral Thomas O. Selfridge, Jr., the house commands its location overlooking the East Passage of Narragansett Bay, and offered its owner a view of all the ships passing by and at anchor. The house reads as a castle from afar, and a masterwork of complex forms and shingled surfaces up close.

100. *The Barnacle*. Photo, ca. 1915. Jamestown Historical Society. The photo documents the increasing treescape surrounding The Barnacle by the early 1900s. Admiral Selfridge enjoyed a majestic view of the U.S. Fleet assembled in the East Passage of Narragansett Bay. Thomas O. Selfridge, Sr. and Jr. had the distinction of being the first father and son with the rank of rear admiral while both serving in the U.S. Navy.

101. *The Barnacle*. Photo, ca. 1900. Jamestown Historical Society. The inventive quality of Bevins's concept for The Barnacle is one of fusing various shapes together and unifying them in a harmonious shingled surface. The band of windows for the stairwell is the most striking element of the facade.

102. William Gilder. *View of the Barnacle from the North*. Photo, ca. 1900. Jamestown Historical Society.

103. *View of The Barnacle* [left] *and Joseph S. Lovering Cottage* [right] *from Dumpling Drive*. Photo, ca. 1900. Rosengarten Album. Jamestown Historical Society. The houses along Dumpling Drive and in the Ocean Highlands district, built in a flurry of activity during the 1880s, were set within the fields and grasslands that had been cultivated since colonial settlement and occupation by the Narragansett tribe. These new dwellings of the 1880s were inspired by the simplicity and time-worn patina of rocky coast and grassy meadow. The talent of the architect's work, namely Charles L. Bevins, was to take the inherent natural features of the land and create an architecture immersed in the land and rising from it at the same time.

104. *Sitting on the Porch at The Barnacle*. Photo, ca. 1895. Jamestown Historical Society. Bevins used his characteristic curved and shingle-clad porch openings at The Barnacle, creating an environment of textured wooden surfaces framing views of cove and bay.

105. Mary Remey Wadleigh. *Admirals of Jamestown*. Photo, 1903. Jamestown Historical Society. From left to right: Rear Admiral Thomas O. Selfridge, Sr., Rear Admiral Thomas O. Selfridge, Jr., and Rear Admiral George C. Remey. This photo was taken by Rear Admiral Remey's daughter at The Barnacle. Rear Admiral Thomas O. Selfridge, Sr., was ninety-seven years of age. He died the following year, at ninety-eight. Jamestown appealed to naval personnel and was home to over thirty officers, ranking from admiral to captain, in the late nineteenth and twentieth centuries. From the porches of their summer houses, leading naval figures could watch gatherings of the U.S. Fleet in the East Passage of Narragansett Bay.

but Selfridge was acquitted at a court martial in 1888.[81] His career did not appear to suffer, since he rose to the rank of rear admiral in 1896 while serving as commander in chief of the European Squadron of the U.S. Navy (1895–98). A Veteran Companion of the Military Order of the Loyal Legion of the United States and an Honorary Hereditary Companion of the Military Orders of Foreign Wars—honors he had in common with his father—Selfridge Jr. was also a Knight of the French Legion of Honor.[82] The figure of Selfridge and the form of his house seemed to be very much in sympathy, each a towering presence:

> *… the beautiful summer residence of Captain Thomas O. Selfridge, U. S. N. It is perched directly on top of a huge rock on the water's edge, and commands an unobstructed view of Newport, War College, Training Station, Torpedo Station, Fort Adams, Old Fort Dumplings… . It measures 61 x 42 feet and so completely covers its natural foundation that a man cannot walk on the rock… . There are also two handsome loggias in the second story, one on the north-east corner and one on the south-west corner, and from an open balcony on the north-west corner can be obtained a view over the island and out to sea… . A pier extends out over the water from the first story a distance of about one hundred feet, with a bathhouse at the end for deep-water bathing… . The top of the rock on which this unique structure is built was blasted off to make a level foundation. The place is very appropriately christened "The Barnacle." It was not for want of land that Capt. Selfridge chose to put his house upon a rock, as the site has thirty acres.*[83]

Rear Admiral Selfridge could view the vast expanse of shimmering water below his house. The Barnacle was his lookout upon dramatic natural scenery, including Fort Dumpling with historic associations, and views of the comings and goings of a pageant of ships, both naval and commercial.

The Boulders (1888) is also the product of a military patron, but the army rather than the navy. Charles Larned, a professor of art at West Point, commissioned this large cottage, attributed to Charles Bevins. Nearby stood the houses of fellow artists James B. Sword and William Trost Richards. Unusually deep porches characterize The Boulders, creating outdoor rooms and allowing the house to function as an airy pavilion (Fig. 106). Few moldings and no ornament disrupt the even flow of the shingled surfaces as they travel along flat walls, around tall windows, around a large central dormer topped by a triangular pediment and the juxtaposition of small bands of windows with large-scale openings. The service wing is slightly lower than the main house and terminates with an angled gable known as a "jerkinhead," derived from medieval northern European rural architecture.

Charles Larned's neighbor, James B. (Brade) Sword, built his cottage in 1883. Unlike larger houses in the area, this design is focused less on wood and the encompassing porch, giving it the open-air quality of an East Asian bungalow. Railings for the porch fuse Queen Anne Revival and Japanesque motifs, with the parts of the house as interconnected squares, all under a slanted roof (Figs. 107 and 109). The bases of the porch foundation walls are angled, and with the rest

106. *The Boulders*. Photo, ca. 1900. Meredith and Clarke Album. Jamestown Historical Society. The Boulders was built in 1888 by Charles Bevins for Charles Larned, professor of art at West Point. Fellow artists James B. Sword and William Trost Richards lived nearby. Bevins displays a subtle understanding of scale in The Boulders. Many of his key features are used, namely the bell-capped tower: here used as a second-story bay window (right side of house). The arched openings of the porch create a steady visual effect for the entrance to the house, and the side wing (left) encompassing service and kitchen wings is masterfully composed with a second-floor bracket supporting the roof, which lowers in grade into the next roofline terminating in a jerkinhead gable.

107. *James B. Sword House*. Photo, 1888. Jamestown Historical Society. Built in 1883 to a design attributed to James Sword, this house embraces a dominant abstraction in its forms. The absolute austerity of the roof, bold in its outline, and the delicacy of the Japanese-inspired porch railing is a compelling combination. Surrounded by vast fields, the simplicity of the house complements its surroundings, blending into the grassy meadows in tone and texture of its shingled surfaces.

108. *Joseph S. Lovering Cottage.* Photo, ca. 1900. Meredith and Clarke Album. Jamestown Historical Society. Bevins adheres to greater symmetry of composition in this project, compared to his other Conanicut projects. Built in 1889, the central gable is complemented directly below by two smaller triangular pediments on the porch. Wood shingles unify the entire exterior, and the siting of the house is characteristic of the architect's use of the contours of the land. Bevins sets the building within the rock outcroppings and perches the right side of it on the edge of the cliffs, so the building's profile from roof to porch leads the eye naturally to the rocky angle of the coastline.

of the building create a series of seamlessly integrated stepped pyramidal slopes from shingled base to porch and roof. From his studio, Sword captured the textures and light of Conanicut in canvases depicting the land, coast, and its aged farmhouses.

Grey Ledge (1895) introduced an architect of supreme talent and subtlety to Jamestown in Wilson Eyre, Jr., a Philadelphia-based designer known for his decidedly informal plans and minimalist approach to wood-shingled compositions. These characteristics are clearly present in his house for Eliza Alexander, the first of the cottages on Beavertail, the windswept grassy knoll of Conanicut's southern tip.[84] The clean, crisp rectangular form of the house with its overhanging roof and central arch are simple and straightforward, without complex gables or additions. At the center is a large-scale arch with shingles curving around its edges. The simplicity

109. *James B. Sword House*. Photo, 1888. Jamestown Historical Society. Surrounded by vast fields, the simplicity of the house complements its surroundings, blending into the grassy meadows in tone and texture of its shingled surfaces.

and solidity of the building effectively addresses the site, taking on the high winds and blending with the waving grasses that surround it. Integration of house with landscape formed a key component of Eyre's work and his writing as he emerged as a leading figure in the country life movement both at home and abroad. He was one of the founders of *House and Garden* magazine (1901) and was also one of the first U.S. architects to be featured in influential publications, specifically the British Arts and Crafts magazine *International Studio* and in the German book *Das englische Haus* (The English House, 1904) by Hermann Muthesius.[85]

The Case of Charles Bevins

"Hundreds of summer cottages have been built within the past two years, ranging in cost from 8,500 to 680,000, and Charles L. Bevins, the architect, is working night and day to furnish plans for others to be erected for next season."

"Jamestown," *Newport Mercury*, June 30, 1888

THE ENIGMATIC FIGURE OF CHARLES BEVINS looms large on Conanicut. With an office in Newport and a residence in Jamestown, Bevins made a significant mark on the look of the island with a series of residences drawing upon the prevailing Queen Anne, Shingle, and Colonial Revival styles.[86] These styles of architecture, notable for their asymmetrical forms, open floor plans, generous porches, and materials and ornamental vocabulary derived from a variety of sources ranging from the English and European medieval to the Japanese and the colonial American, inspired much of the resort architecture on the coast and in the mountains of the United States beginning in the 1870s. Equally popular in the cities and burgeoning suburbs, these picturesque houses expressed the search for a unique American identity in architecture. In nearby Newport, established as one of the most fashionable seaside resorts in the nation, architects such as New York–based McKim, Mead and White and the Boston firm of Peabody and Stearns articulated their versions of a vernacular-inspired architectural idiom that has come to be known as the "Shingle Style," but, at the time, was referred to as the "modernized colonial," a very appropriate term for the working methods of the architects who freely drew upon historic features to produce contemporary designs.[87] In 1881, Bevins entered this scene and began working for Peabody and Stearns,[88] architects renowned for their rusticated stone summer estate, Vinland (1882), with a shingled hen house, both noted for their grandly proportioned entrance arches, in Newport for Catharine Lorillard Wolfe, and for Kragsyde (1883–1885), a house with yet another massive shingled arch perched on the rocky shoreline of Manchester-by-the-Sea, Massachusetts. These projects provided a formula for bold design elements and planning that infuses Bevins's later work.

The influence of the picturesque, its asymmetrical massing of forms, the exaggeration of proportions, the appreciation of rough-hewn materials, and vernacular models from a variety of sources, play out in the Jamestown buildings attributed to Bevins. Through his association with Peabody and Stearns, and with access to the burgeoning architectural press featuring Queen Anne Revival, Shingle Style, and Colonial Revival houses, Bevins had access to numerous sources to aid his own imagination. Unlike his contemporaries practicing in the bright lights of Newport, where *Munsey's Magazine* reported that "society is always on dress parade," with many new buildings often illustrated, photographed, and featured in the press, Bevins practiced in relative

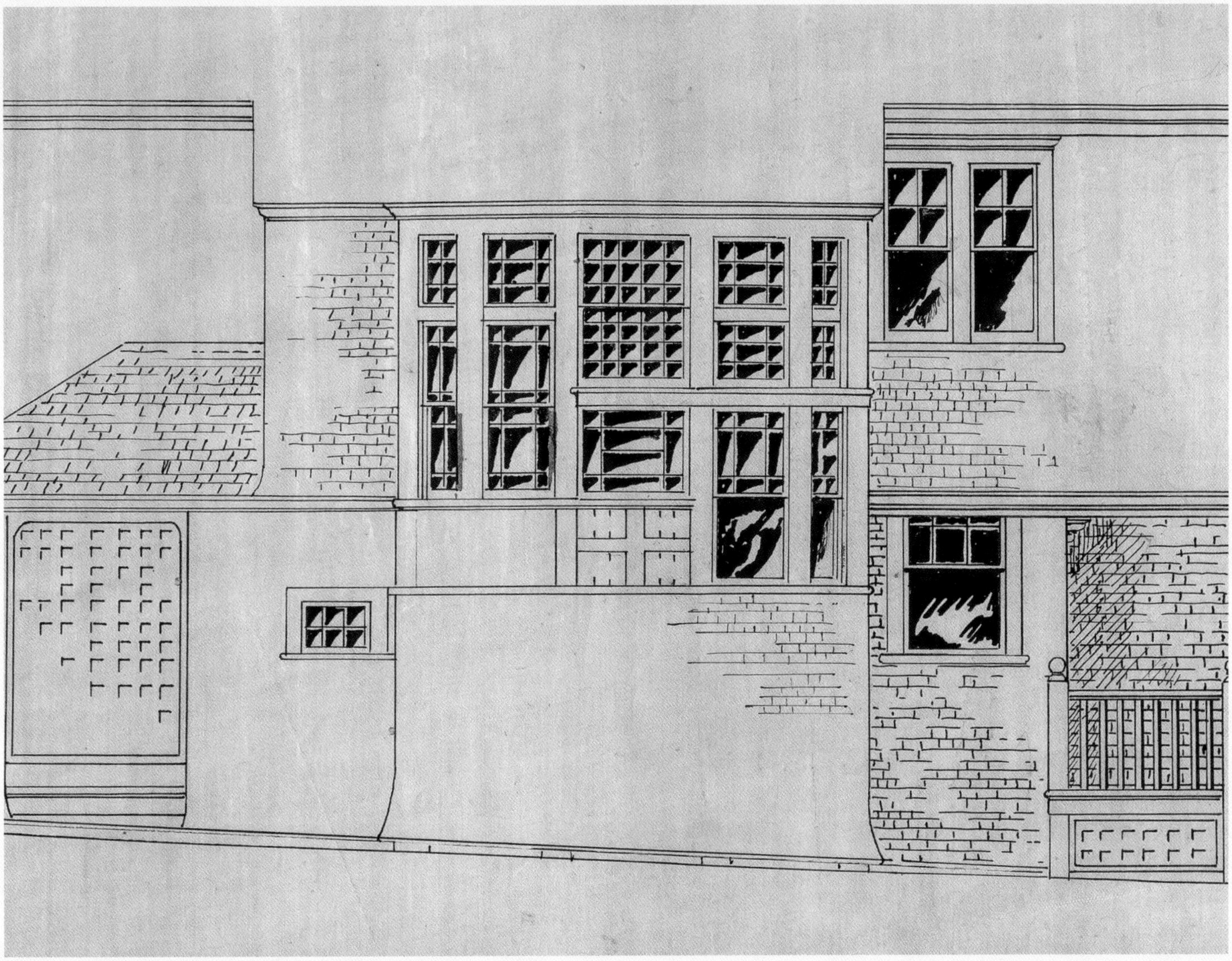

South Elevation, Faris House (detail), 1895. Jamestown Historical Society.

obscurity, leaving few drawings behind, and commissioned by clients who opted for the serenity and privacy of Jamestown.[89] His existing signed drawings reveal his office address in Newport, so he did see all of the architectural goings-on, and these renderings establish a series of architectural forms and features that are evident in other buildings attributed to Bevins (Figs. 110–16), forming a substantial portfolio of work from his private residences for Philadelphia families to the Thorndike Hotel (1889), St. Mark's Episcopal Church (1892), and the Moveable Chapel of the Transfiguration (1899).[90] The

110. *Faris House*. Photo, ca. 1900. Jamestown Historical Society. Designed by Bevins for Charles A. Faris and built in 1895 by the Jamestown-based contractor Peter Knowles. Bevins created strong lines in this house, with a sharp-angled gambrel roof with wide moldings. The porch posts are also substantial vertical elements, while atop the porch roof is a shingled balcony that integrates into the roofline.

111. *North Elevation, Faris House*. Drawing, dated "1895" or "1896" in pencil. Jamestown Historical Society. The large gable encapsulating the smaller gable defines this facade, and the true masterstroke of design is the gentle outward curve of the second-floor balcony, clad in shingles. This balcony projects on the right in order to visually keep in line with the small gable projecting behind it.

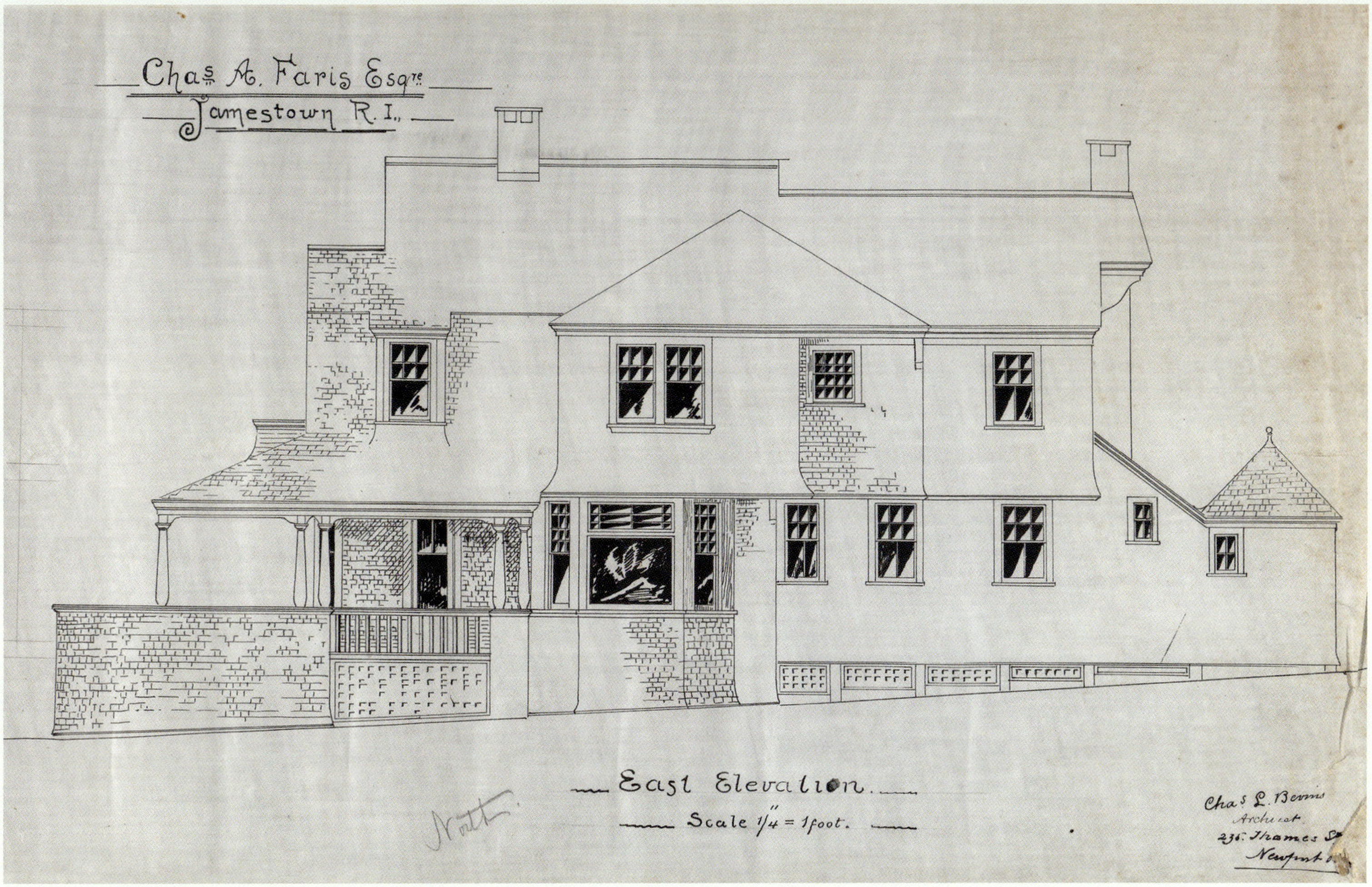

112. *East Elevation, Faris House*. Drawing, ca. 1895. Jamestown Historical Society. The drawing of the east elevation reveals a complex arrangement of forms: a large porch, an asymmetrical roofline, a bay window, and a one-story pitched roof structure (far right). Bevins's disciplined approach is evident in the central section of the facade with its triangular roof under which he arranges a set of paired windows (left) terminating in a curved wall that links into the bay window below. To the right of the paired second-story windows is a recessed area with a smaller square-paned window. A large curved bracket is at the very end of the facade (far right), a detail seen in many of Bevins's houses. In this drawing, one sees the architect working with a series of geometric forms, all unified by gentle curves to link each section of the facade.

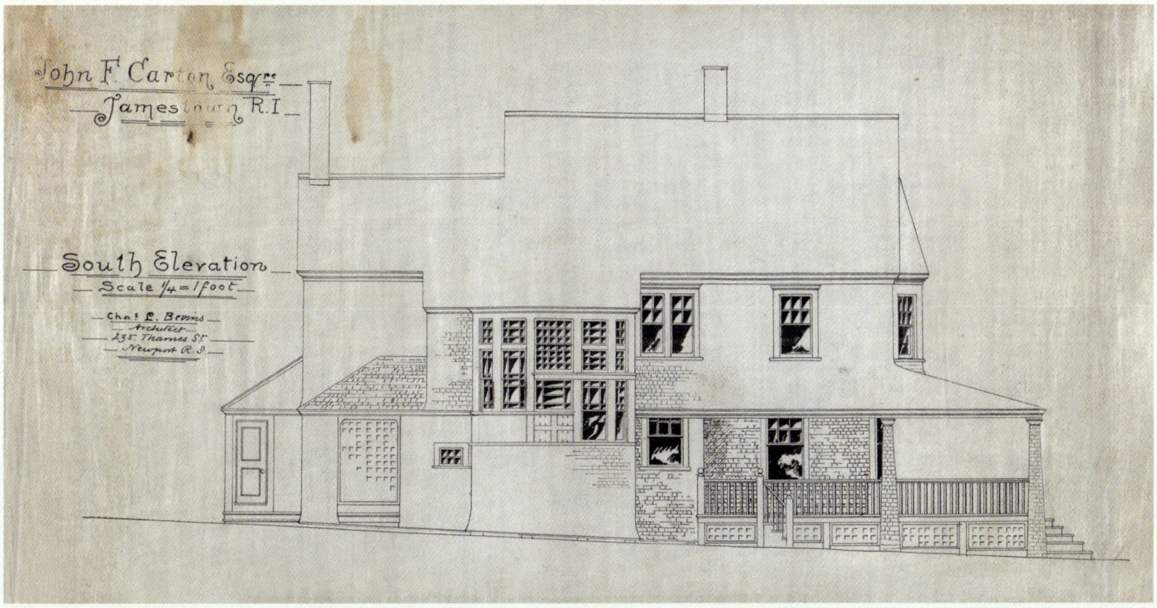

113. *South Elevation, Faris House*. Drawing, ca. 1895. Jamestown Historical Society. The south elevation has an upper wall of windows reminiscent of the stairwell windows of The Barnacle, designed by Bevins in 1886.

Faris and Carton house drawings, signed by Bevins, provide valuable insights into his choice of design elements (Figs. 111–14). Each building features interlocking gables that give an overall structure and harmony to the facades. While the Faris house has a slanted gambrel roof encompassing the gables, Bevins opted for steep triangular gables for the Carton residence. The architect focuses on the integration of geometric shapes, specifically the triangle, to bring discipline to complex compositions of porches, bay windows, dormers, projecting wings, and rooflines. Of particular note is the band of windows on the Carton house facade, which also appear on The Barnacle.

In addition to his picturesque schemes, Bevins also embraced the more classically oriented Colonial Revival as it rose in popularity. In 1899, he designed a house for C. W. Bailey, a Philadelphia jeweler in the firm of Bailey, Banks and Biddle, derived from eighteenth-century classical Georgian prototypes, relying more upon a symmetrical form with a Palladian window rather than the complexity of his earlier shingled cottages.

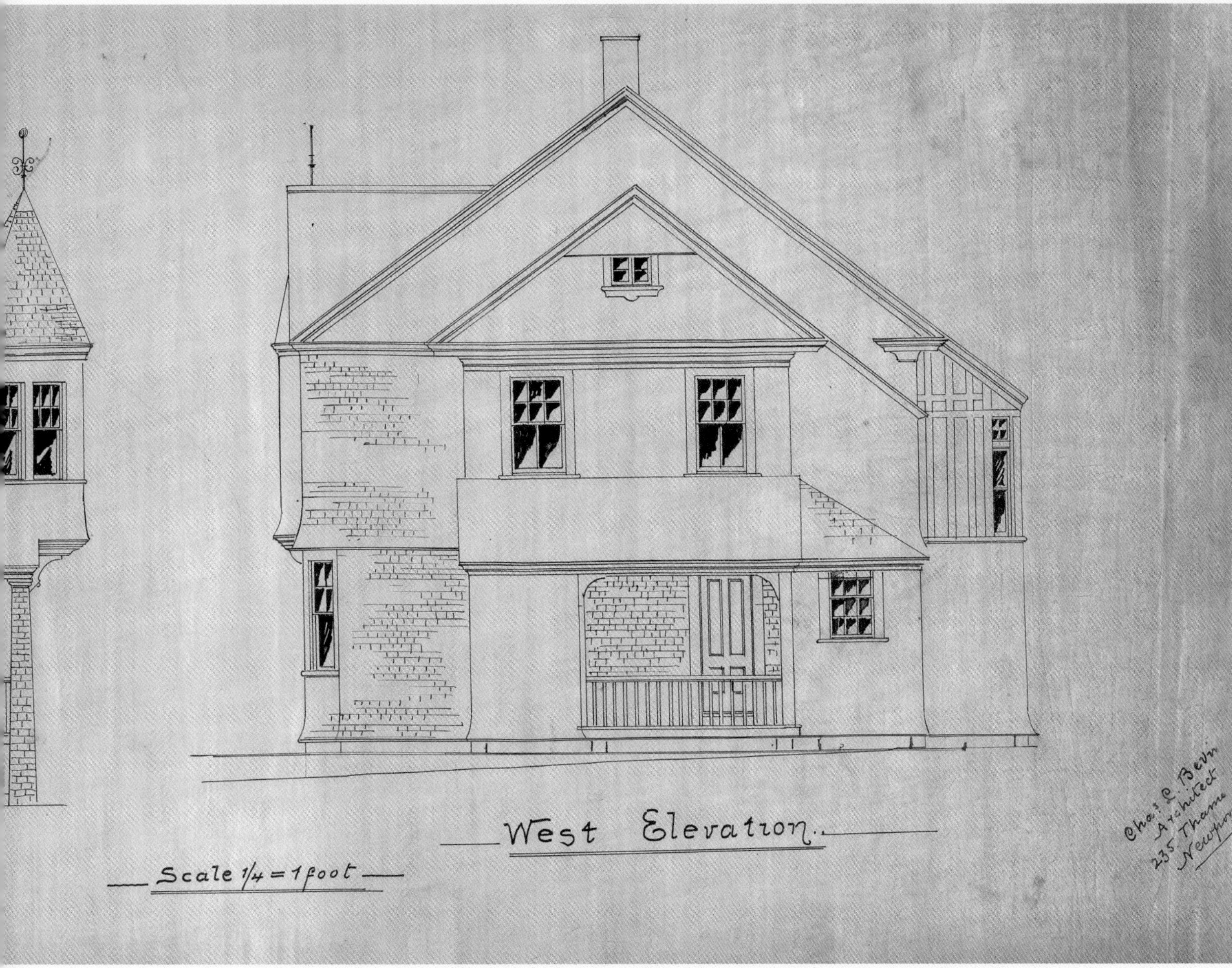

114. *East and West Elevations, Carton House*. Drawing, dated "1895" in pencil. Jamestown Historical Society. These facades represent Bevins working in both complex and simple compositions. The east elevation, used as a main entrance, is rich in large-scale porch posts and a second-floor corner turret (right), while the west elevation is a study in retrained architectural forms, of gables within gables all in a carefully controlled scheme for this servants' entrance.

ICE CREAM & CONFECTIONERY
NEWPORT DAILY NEWS

115. *Thorndike Hotel*. Photo, ca. 1900. Jamestown Historical Society. While Bevins worked well with complex rooflines, he truly triumphed in many of his works with simplicity, specifically at the Thorndike Hotel with its continuous unadorned shingled surface, bringing harmony to the expansive scale of the facade, punctuated by his signature curved porch openings.

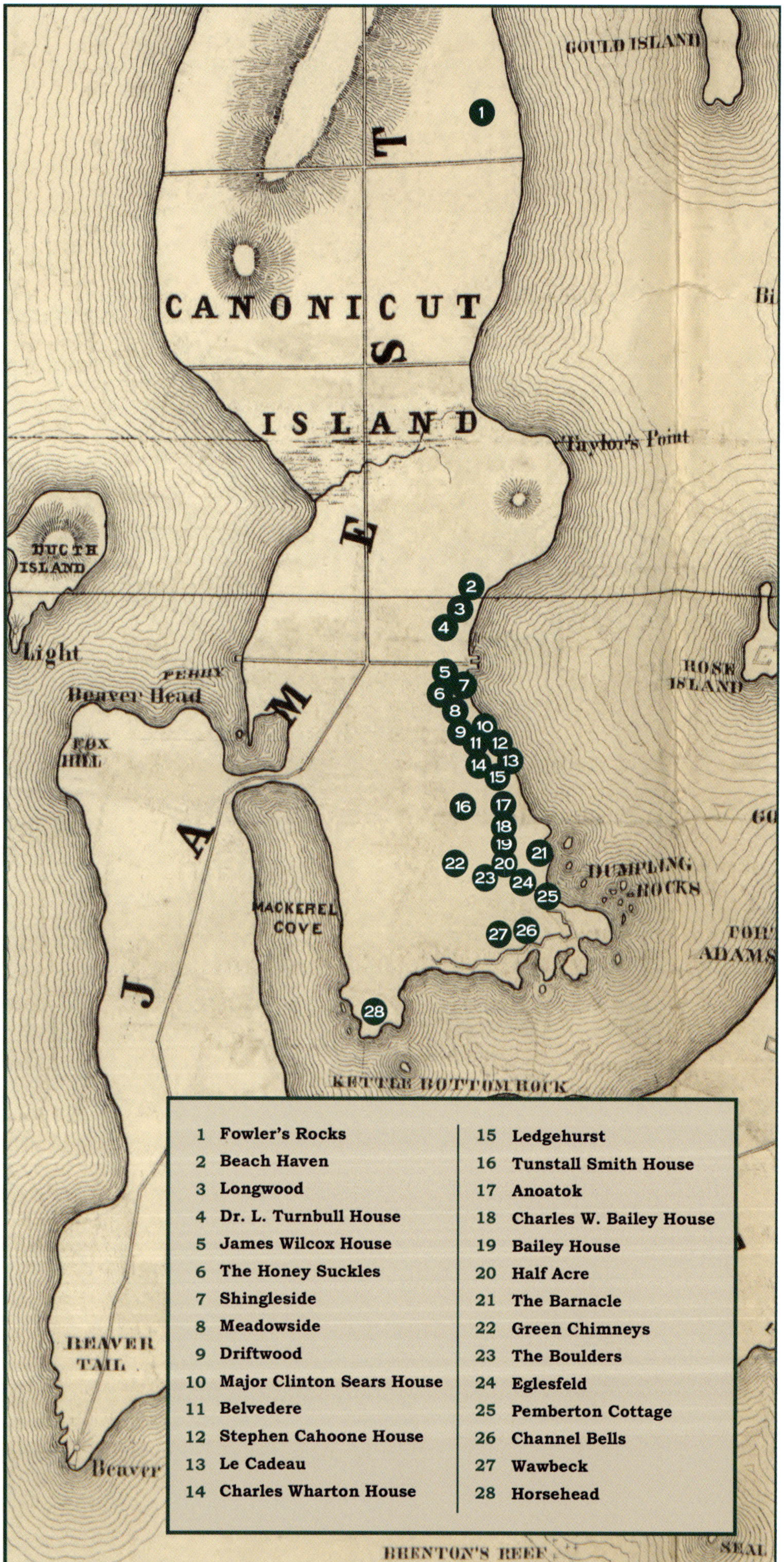

116. Detail from Henry Francis Walling's *Map of Newport County, Rhode Island*, 1850 (Library of Congress, Washington, D.C.) showing the existing houses on Conanicut Island by architect Charles L. Bevins. Design: Barbara Shea and Charles McGowan.

CLINGSTONE: PICTURESQUE ON THE ROCKS

Rock, waves, wind, and very little land comprise the extraordinary undertaking known as Clingstone, a house defying the odds in construction and exposure to the forces of nature. Joseph Lovering Wharton, a nephew of Joseph Wharton of nearby Horsehead, lost his house, Stornaway, to the U.S. government to make way for Fort Wetherill, so he hired Newport architect J. D. Johnston to realize his vision of a shingled retreat on a dumpling, one of the rock outcroppings in the East Passage. Between 1904 and 1906, building materials were ferried across the bay. Noted as an efficient and effective builder, Johnston operated his own mill in Newport and provided the heavy mill framing anchored to the rock as reinforcement against hurricane-force gales.[91] The rustic quality of the house is evident in the use of exterior shingles for interior spaces, with burlap-covered ceilings and beach-pebble fireplaces (Figs. 117–21). Large windows offered panoramic views and were made of the type of heavy plate glass used for ship portholes. Since the windows weighed too much to be easily moved, hatches in the walls provided ventilation.[92] Never was a house more integrated with its setting. Clingstone clings to its rock and appears to float on water, catching every breeze and ocean mist that Narragansett Bay cares to send.

117. *Clingstone.* Photo, ca. 1905. Jamestown Historical Society.

118. *Clingstone*. Photo, ca. 1950. Jamestown Historical Society. In 1903 Joseph Samuel Lovering Wharton engaged Charles L. Bevins to design Clingstone on one of the dumplings, the rocky outcroppings, in the East Passage of Narragansett Bay, within site of the Conanicut cottages of his extended family relations. The house is a feat of engineering and construction, overseen by J. D. Johnston.

119. *Clingstone, Living Room*. Photo, 1904. Jamestown Historical Society.

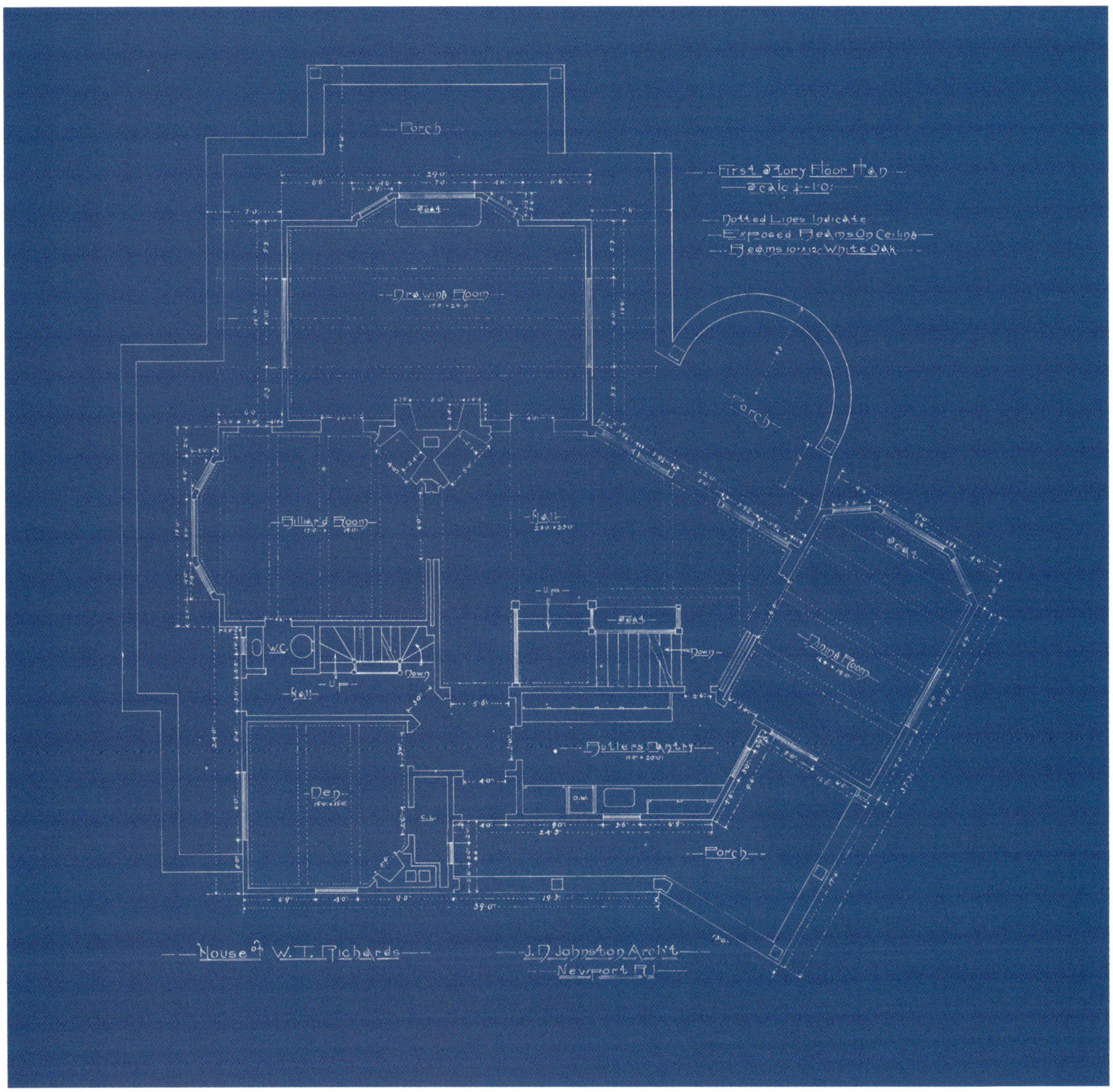

120. *Clingstone, Floor Plan*. Photo, 1903. Rhode Island Historical Society. The plan is focused on rooms angled to take advantage of sweeping views of Narragansett Bay. Note that the plan states it is the residence of William Trost Richards, who initially may have intended to live on the dumpling, but the project was eventually taken over by J. S. Lovering.

121. *Clingstone, Facade*. Drawing, 1903. Rhode Island Historical Society. The massive stone foundations of Clingstone are a testament to J. D. Johnston's skill in construction, even in the most challenging environments. The result of Bevins's design and Johnston's engineering is a tour de force of architecture meeting nature.

EDWARD MITCHELL BANNISTER: AN AMERICAN MASTER ON THE SHORES OF CONANICUT

A MASTER OF ATMOSPHERIC PASTORAL landscapes, Edward Mitchell Bannister excelled with his brush in rendering nature in its timeless appeal. Born in St. Andrews in New Brunswick, Canada, his heritage part West Indian, part Canadian, he emigrated to Boston where he studied photography and portraiture, read classical literature, and viewed the landscapes of the American painter William Morris Hunt, who had spent time with the coterie of French artists such as Jean-François Millet and Jean-Baptiste-Camille Corot at Barbizon exploring the effects of light and color. The misty, light-filled canvases of these artists would have a profound effect on Bannister's own aesthetic and technical development as he moved easily from soft tones to lush colors in his work.[93] He met Christiana Carteaux in Boston when applying as a barber in her shop. Born in Rhode Island, Carteaux was of African and Narragansett descent. She and Bannister were married in 1857 and became active members in artistic circles and in the abolitionist movement. In 1869, the couple moved to Providence, Rhode Island, where Bannister, with his wife's support, devoted himself full time to his art. Sailing on the waters of Narragansett Bay, exploring the rivers and marshy inlets of the coastline, Bannister practiced and perfected his approach to landscape painting. Awarded a Bronze Medal at the Philadelphia Centennial of 1876, Bannister ranks as the first Black artist to win a national prize in the United States. His pastoral landscape *Under the Oaks* received acclaim, although once his race became known, the jurors attempted to withdraw the award.

"He becomes the interpreter of the infinite, subtle qualities of the spiritual idea centering in all created things, expounding for us the laws of beauty ... revealing to us glimpses of the absolute idea of perfect harmony."

Edward Mitchell Bannister,
lecture on the role of the artist, 1886

122. A. Gergner. *Edward Mitchell Bannister and Companions*. Photo, 1887. Newport Historical Society. P39.

Fairness prevailed when fellow artists at the exhibition protested. Bannister received his well-earned Bronze Medal. As his reputation grew locally and nationally, he was invited to serve on the founding board of the Rhode Island School of Design in 1878, and he co-founded the Providence Art Club in 1880 with fellow artists.[94] When he came upon Conanicut in summer, Bannister found the qualities of light, water, color, and topography to fill his canvases (Fig. 122). Colorful and bold brushwork enlivens *Fort Dumpling* (1890), his rendition of the historic monument with people enjoying the grassy hillside abounding in high grass and flowers with the sea beyond. In *Jamestown Harbor at Sunset* (1895), Bannister captures the calm of the water at day's end and treats the paint in impressionist brushstrokes (Fig. 123). Humanity and the spirit of place informs his works, and imbues color, light, and stillness into his compositions. Boats rest at harbor, the land is solid and eternal.

Following pages:
123. Edward Mitchell Bannister. *Jamestown Harbor at Sunset*. Oil on canvas, 1895. Jamestown Historical Society.

THE ROMANCE OF THE PAST: THE COLONIAL REVIVAL AND JAMESTOWN

> *"[E]very night I go to sleep in the old four poster bed hoping her ghost will come. I hear the old trumpet vine rapping and tapping on the window."*
>
> Harry Carr on the Carr Homestead in the *Los Angeles Times*, 1925

HARRY CARR'S WORDS REVEAL A romanticism inspired by the Colonial Revival movement of the late nineteenth and early twentieth centuries. This is the critical connection between colonial Jamestown of farm and field and the romantic Jamestown of the Victorian age. One period informed the other, and it is an engaging story of characters and their creativity in reimagining the island of Conanicut. The 1876 Centennial generated a great surge of interest in American history. These sentiments also sparked the multi-dimensional Colonial Revival, which influenced art, architecture, design, literature, and the preservation of historic sites. As architect Robert S. Peabody declared in 1876: "With our Centennial year have we not discovered that we too have a past worthy of study?"[95] The awareness of Jamestown's colonial heritage prompted a whole range of interests and shaped the future of the island. Across the United States, the Colonial Revival affected an entire universe of both professionals and amateurs in a variety of fields motivated by the idea of an identifiable American past. Architects, landscape designers, painters, sculptors, photographers, writers, and historians formed the vanguard of this movement, seeking out and documenting historic sites. The architect Charles Follen McKim commissioned the earliest known portfolio of photographs of colonial buildings and objects of interest in Newport in 1872 by the internationally renowned artist William James Stillman.[96] These images documented the past but they also served McKim's contemporary design work. Herein is the essence of the Colonial Revival, an approach to the past that embraced both fact and fiction. One could preserve a colonial farmhouse and save a painting and spinning wheel with respect for its authentic forms, or one could interpret these sources and add even more colonial-inspired frippery to them. Both approaches had their merits. Some have stood the test of time better than others, but whether fact-based or fantasy-driven, both encouraged an appreciation of a bygone era, for good or ill. Jamestown's history wore itself openly in fields and surviving stone walls, farmhouses, and the earthworks remaining from military batteries. Most pre-Revolutionary era structures had been destroyed by the British or were encased in later additions,

124. *Carr Homestead*. Photo, 1921. Lena Clarke Album. Jamestown Historical Society. The house engulfed in vines only heightened its romantic appeal, along with its original date of construction in 1776, making it a Colonial Revival icon.

but beautifully proportioned late eighteenth-century dwellings, a meeting house, and a windmill survived and were viewed as icons in the landscape (Figs. 124 and 125).

The Thomas Paine House, known as Cajacet, is a site where the reality of the colonial and the romance of its revival come together. In 1882, the Providence and Boston art dealer Seth Vose acquired the house as his summer estate. He set to remodeling the structure, adding dormers and patterned shingles in the popular Queen Anne mode (Figs. 128–31). It is an entirely decorative fantasy, the outline of an ancient house with connections to a colonial antique, updated as a seasonal retreat.[97]

FARMHOUSE TO COLONIAL REVIVAL ICON: THE CARR FAMILY HOMESTEAD

THE CARR FAMILY OF JAMESTOWN, WITH ancestors as founders of the English settlement, colonial governors, and long-standing prominent members of the community, came to be living emblems of the Colonial Revival. Their theatricals in eighteenth-century costume and the guise of historic figures became legendary (Fig. 126). Set against the vine-covered family homestead, these gatherings reinforced the value of Jamestown's colonial origins. Harry Carr immersed himself in his family's history and lore while spending the summer of 1925 at the house, musing on the ghosts of the past, dwelling on the spirit of his great-grandmother, who lived in the Carr Homestead in the early 1800s, writing,

> *Her name was Mary Cross. I imagine that her marriage must have been quite a society affair. Her husband was the great-grandson of old Governor Caleb Carr, who was one of the last of the royal governors of Rhode Island. She was the daughter of a colonel in the Colonial army… . Downstairs is an old clock builded in 1640, which still ticks just as when the sun danced on the water of Narragansett Bay… . My great-grandfather loved her so dearly… . They say that the spirit of Mary Cross comes back by night to this old bedroom—yearning over the little boy and his little sister, struggling to raise the family that she left.*[98]

"Probably the thing that Caleb did that had the most lasting effect upon the family was his purchase of large tracts of land on the island of Conanicut (Jamestown). Here several of his children took up their residence, here his descendants still live almost three hundred years afterward. During all that time the Carrs have taken a prominent part in the affairs of the island."

W. L. Watson, *The House of Carr*, 1926

Harry Carr used his ancestral home as a stage for a dream-like reminiscence combining historical data with the misty spirit of place. Both are powerful tools of engagement for readers, the data grounding the experience of the text in the tangible and provable, while the more intangible mood the author creates reinforces deeper personal meaning and cultural interpretation.

Carr's romantic musings were followed the next year, 1926, by W. L. Watson's *The House of Carr*.[99] Watson based the book in historical fact, while the spirit of the publication appeals to the romance of generations rooted in a time-worn place. The author focuses on the origin story of the Carrs and their role as early settlers on the island:

> *In contrast with the forested shores of Aquidnick, Conanicut had some cleared land where the Indians had for generations summered and grown their corn and vegetables. This area of hay, pasturage and vegetable land appealed to the forest bound colonists of Newport. Thus in 1659 we find William Coddington, Benedict Arnold, William Brenton, Caleb Carr and Richard Smith leading a company of Newport citizens in arranging the transfer of Conanicut and the small adjoining islands of Gould and Dutch to themselves.*[100]

In the antiquarian and preservation movements sparked by the Colonial Revival, both the fiction-inspired myth of Harry Carr and the fact-based history of W. L. Watson held equal influence. By definition, antiquarians devote themselves to the study and collecting of objects of the past; preservationists commit themselves to the care of objects of the past. There is a fine line between the two that is often blurred. Preservation generally grew out of antiquarian impulses and also added a strong element of interpreting cultural identity through historic sites (Figs. 127, 132, and 133). One such case on Jamestown is the pivotal moment of saving the only surviving eighteenth-century windmill. Although it no longer fulfilled a practical need after it closed in 1876, the structure became a landmark, a site of memory as evident in a formation in 1904 of the Windmill Society. Mrs. Frank H. Remington penned the society's appeal to preserve the mill, writing, "Not only is it an object of beauty in itself and a fine specimen of a type of building very rare in this country, but it one of the few remaining links which bind us to the past, and almost the only object of interest of which Jamestown can boast."[101] In 1912, the deed for the mill was transferred to the newly created Jamestown Historical Society. The island now had its own identity, for some, embedded in a historic monument.

125. *Carr Homestead Fireplace*. Photo, 1947. Merrill Smith Collection. Jamestown Historical Society.

126. *Carr Theatricals*. Photo, ca. 1926. Jamestown Historical Society.

127. James B. Sword. *Weeden House.* Watercolor, 1882. Jamestown Historical Society. Sword also captured the ancient atmosphere preserved in Conanicut's old farmhouses, resting at ease among their fields.

128. *Mr. and Mrs. Seth Vose and Family on the Lawn at Cajacet*. Photo, ca. 1882. Jamestown Historical Society. On the back of the photograph is a note stating that the house was "built in 1690 by the privateer Thomas Paine."

129. *Exterior, Cajacet.* Photo, ca. 1943. Jamestown Historical Society.

130. *Roof Gables and Shingles of Cajacet* (detail). Photo, ca. 1885. Jamestown Historical Society.

The Paine House, Conanicut, R.I.

This is a picturesque old building on Conanicut Park Farm, said to have been built by Capt. Thos. Paine, who married one of Gov. Carr's daughters. It must be about 180 years old. Many silly stories have been told about this place in connection with Capt. Kidd.

The Carr House, Conanicut, R.I.

This is a singular old place, consisting of two buildings, one frame, and the other stone; the latter having an immense stone chimney, and doubtless the older portion. It was probably built by Gov. Carr for his son, nearly 200 years ago.

131. *Homes of Our Forefathers.* Drawing, 1882. Library of Congress.

132. William Trost Richards. *Old House on Conanicut Island*. Watercolor on paper, 1876. Courtesy of the Pennsylvania Academy of the Fine Arts. Gift of Dorrance H. Hamilton in memory of Samuel M. V. Hamilton. Executed in the year of the Centennial, Richards selected this colonial era dwelling on Conanicut for one of his earliest projects on the island. His work tended to focus on the sea and land, and the play of light on each, but here he renders a time-worn house settled into its surrounding stone-strewn farmland, trees and sea in the distance.

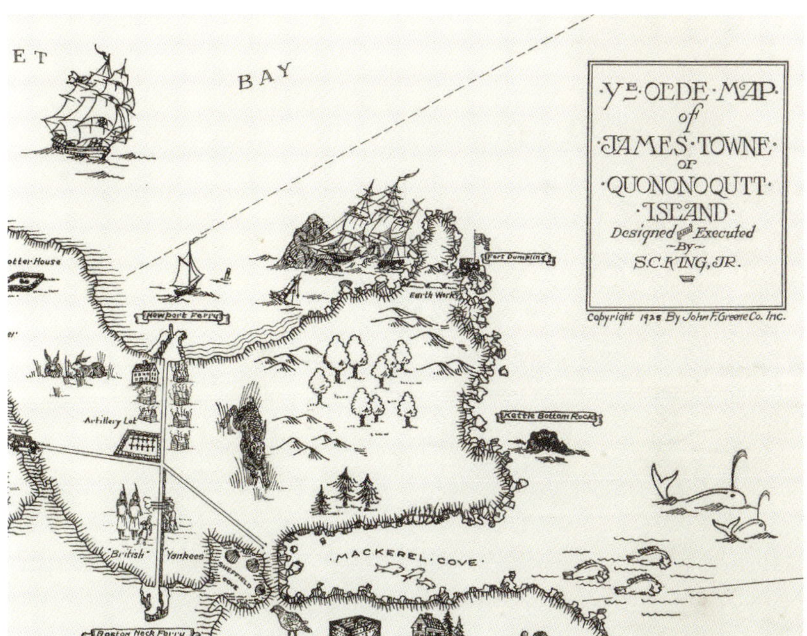

133. Knight. *Map of Jamestown* (detail), ca. 1920. The map is a pictorial extravaganza of Colonial Revival exuberance, noting sites of colonial history rendered in the most romantic fashion.

THE LEGEND OF CAPTAIN KIDD

> *"This is a picturesque old house on Conanicut Park Farm, said to have been built by Capt. Thom. Paine, who married one of Gov. Carr's daughters. It must be about 180 years old. Many silly stories have been told about this place in connection with Capt. Kidd."*
>
> Edwin Whitefield,
> *The Homes of Our Forefathers*, 1882

FEATURED IN A CLASSIC COLONIAL REVIVAL book with a rather patriarchal title, *Homes of Our Forefathers* (1882),[102] the text on Cajacet is telling. Enlivened by connection with an infamous figure of the eighteenth century, Cajacet gave the Vose family retreat a colorful air. Originally the home of Thomas Paine, a pirate and privateer, the house is a solidly built post-and-beam colonial structure associated with a colorful tale. When Paine first arrived in Rhode Island in 1683, he was a pirate known to have raided the Floridian coast. Quaker governor William Coddington, Jr. (1651–1689) approved his privateering commission as valid even though the governors of New York and New Hampshire claimed it was a forgery.[103] Paine made an advantageous match with his marriage to Mercy Carr, daughter of prominent Quaker Caleb Carr, with vast land holdings on Conanicut. He could have led a quiet life in his Jamestown house overlooking calm waters, but one day, Capt Kidd's sloop, *St. Antonio*, carrying ten guns, sailed into the East Passage of Narragansett Bay. According to Samuel Greene Arnold, the British cabinet issued orders to the governors of all colonies to apprehend the "notorious Capt. Kidd should he appear in their waters." According to a letter of July 18, 1699 by Sarah Kidd, her husband sent his boat ashore "with an invitation to Captain Paine to come and see him."[104] Mrs. Kidd supposedly asked Paine to deliver gold to a man named Andrew Knott for Kidd's defense following his arrest.[105] Lord Bellomont, when he visited Newport in 1699, ordered Paine to appear before him, accusing him of receiving stolen goods from Kidd. Paine said that Kidd had asked him to "secure some things for him" but that Paine "refused, alleging my house would be searched and I could not do it."[106] How much is fact and fiction in the legend of Captain Kidd in Narragansett Bay is to be debated by generations of historians. One aspect of the tale is certain. Rhode Island waters were active with the exploits of officially sanctioned privateers and illegally operating pirates in the seventeenth century and into the eighteenth. The legend of Captain Kidd may have been embellished, but it served to enhance the local lore of Conanicut. Kidd and his acquaintance with Thomas Paine remained so strong that the pirate is featured on a 1920s illustrated map of Conanicut, itself a document of the romance that infused the Colonial Revival (Fig. 134).

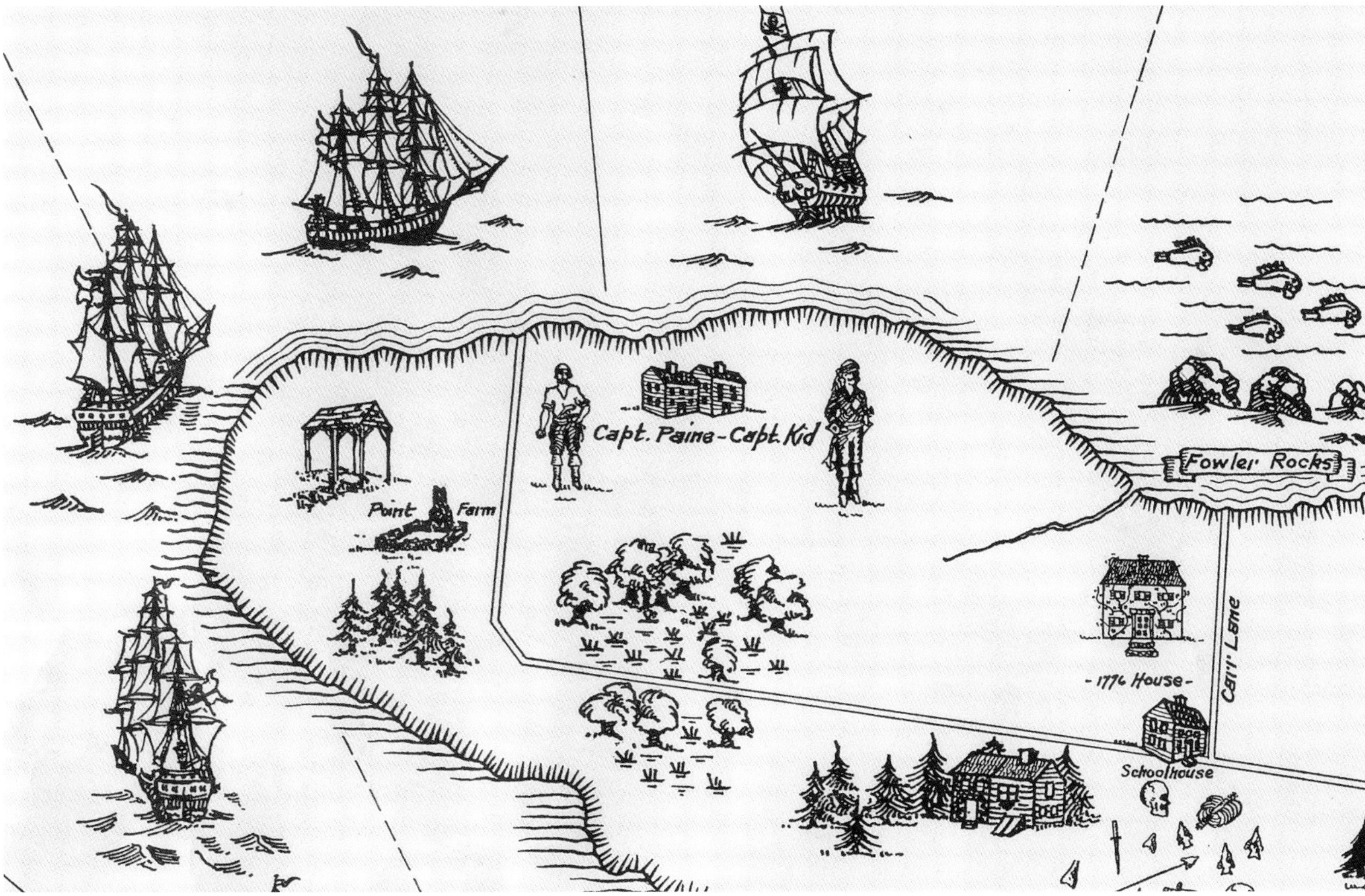

134. Knight. *Map of Jamestown* (detail), ca. 1920. Captain Kidd, regardless of factual data, became celebrated for his association with the Jamestown privateer Thomas Paine. Legends of his buried treasure on Conanicut fueled Colonial Revival legends and lore about the island.

THE ROMANCE OF A ROUND HOUSE

THE ROUND HOUSE (1888) BUILT FOR Philadelphian Daniel S. Newhall, an agent for the Pennsylvania Railroad and a renowned sportsman and cricket player, is a unique expression of Colonial Revival sentiments. Its shape mimics that of Fort Dumpling seen in the distance (Figs. 135 and 136) on a rocky point in the East Passage. Mentioned in the earliest accounts of the region by Giovanni da Verrazzano, mounted with artillery during the War for Independence, and the site of the round stone tower erected in 1799, the old fort starred as one of the most popular sites on Conanicut, appealing to those fascinated by the past and lured by the picturesque. Mr. Newhall's castle-like tower reigned over sweeping views of fields, fort, and the houses of his fellow summer residents.

Fort Dumpling was destroyed on November 26, 1898 and on or near its immediate site rose Fort Wetherill, but its status as a landmark had inspired innumerable paintings and its successor in the Round House. The building has been attributed to McKim, Mead and White, although no documentation confirms this as fact and the structure is unlike any produced by the architects. Newhall would have known of the architects' work in Newport in the 1880s and, in 1891, McKim, Mead and White designed the Colonial Revival–style Cricket Club in Germantown, Pennsylvania, of which Newhall was a member. Although such architectural luminaries cannot be categorically linked with the Round Tower, it remains significant in and of itself, as a bold statement in the land referencing a historic icon:

"[A] peculiar residence, not yet complete, for Mr. Newhall of Philadelphia ... stands upon the side of a huge rock… . Outside staircases lead to the first and second stories. The top of the strange building is perfectly flat and will be used as a lookout. The location is about one hundred yards from the water."

"Jamestown," *Newport Mercury*, June 30, 1888

> *[W]e pass the famous Dumplings, that singular formation of knob-like hillocks, upon a projecting member of which a venerable round fort assumed for many years all the dignity of an important military work. At present the old defences are more picturesque than terrible, and whatever warlike suggestion this particular one may once have offered is now usurped by more modern engineering devices in the vicinity.*[107]

The past had taken on a romantic, theatrical quality in the reimagining of Fort Dumpling, a historic site bathed in nostalgia for a dreamy land of industrious farmers, intrepid seamen, and heroes of revolution. Painted and photographed by artists, celebrated by writers and poets, Fort Dumpling became a monument to the island inhabitants and visitors alike.

135. William Gilder. *Round House*. Photo, ca. 1900. Jamestown Historical Society. The Daniel S. Newhall cottage, built 1888, is in a round shape to mirror the historic Fort Dumpling within its viewshed.

136. William Gilder. *Fort Dumpling*. Photo, ca. 1890. Jamestown Historical Society. Fort Dumpling was built ca. 1800 and demolished 1898.

SHOREBY HILL: THE ROMANTIC VILLAGE REIMAGINED

> *"While Conanicut Island is adorned with many handsome and costly cottages, this is the first effort at scientific and artistic treatment of a larger plot of ground for select summer residences. To this end the owners have secured the services of Ernest W. Bowditch, of Boston, under whose plans and superintendence the work of improvement has been and is being vigorously prosecuted."*
>
> Jamestown Land Company, *Shoreby Hill, Jamestown, RI*, 1896

One passes through rough stone pillars and happens upon the "green" planted with trees and shrubs, an ode to the ideal of the colonial era town common and the appeal of the Victorian park. Shoreby Hill is a combination of the mystique of history and the romance of picturesque scenery: a community of Shingle Style and Colonial Revival houses set in a curvaceous series of roads named after renowned historical and literary figures (Figs. 137–45). It may be seen as the elegant swan song of resort development in Jamestown. The Jamestown Land Company purchased the fifty-eight-acre Greene Farm in 1896 and engaged the civil engineer and landscape designer Ernest Bowditch, working in concert with his brother, James, a forester, to plan the Shoreby Hill plat. This undertaking featured prominent St. Louis financiers and industrialists who had spent many summers in Jamestown. Ephron Catlin, a drug manufacturer, served as Land Company's president, and James Taussig, a lawyer, was its treasurer. Daniel Watson, a Jamestown real estate entrepreneur and descendant of colonial founders of Conanicut, assisted the St. Louis group as local agent. Future St. Louis connected residents included Edward Mallinckrodt, a bank director and owner of chemical plants in several states, and David Francis, who served as mayor of St. Louis, governor of Missouri, secretary of the interior, and ambassador to Russia.[108]

The first subdivision of Shoreby Hill was officially recorded with the Town of Jamestown in September 1898. Within the first week, lots within that plat were sold to purchasers, who had to agree to the following stipulations in order to purchase a property:

1. All buildings were to be at least twenty-two feet from the road.
2. No more than one dwelling house or cottage was to be built on each lot, and exclusively as private residences: not used or occupied as apartments or boarding houses, or for trade or business; no stables were to be erected or maintained, nor cesspools kept.
3. The actual cost of building had to be at least $3,000 unless approved; no fencing or enclosures were to be erected, with the exception of a living hedge, no higher than three and one-half feet in height.
4. The Green was to be common land.
5. All roads were to be private, except Shore Road which is a public highway.
6. After half of the lots had been sold, the owners would become communally responsible for maintenance.
7. There would be annual meetings for collection of dues for upkeep and election of trustees.[109]

Between 1898 and 1936, over sixty houses filled the plots in a street system planned for optimal views of sea and greenery. Ernest Bowditch brought stellar credentials to the project, having recently completed landscape work on the Ochre Point estates of Catharine Lorillard Wolfe, James Van Alen, Pierre Lorillard, and Cornelius Vanderbilt in Newport.[110] In each of these designs, Bowditch devised a picturesque scheme of curving drives and plantings that both concealed and revealed house, grounds, and distant views at given

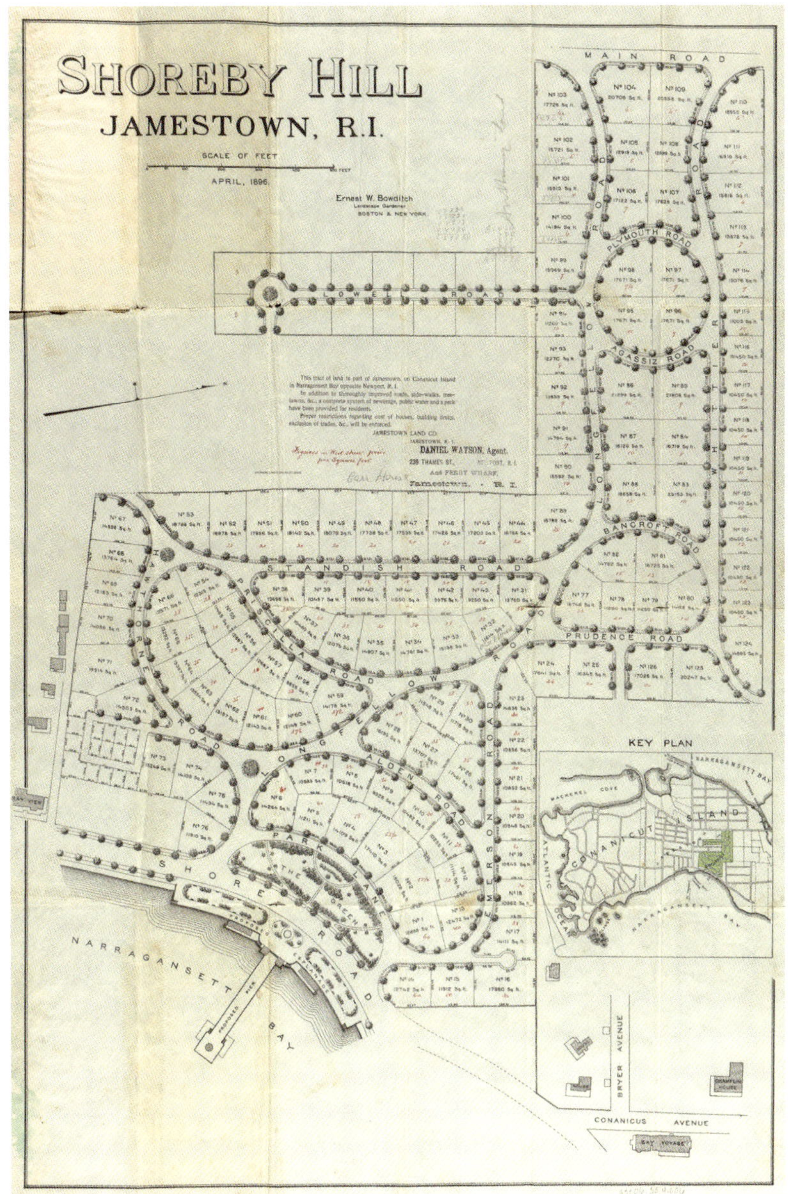

137. Ernest Bowditch. *Plan for Shoreby Hill*, April 1896. Jamestown Historical Society.

ROAD
LON
13934 Sq. ft.
13157 Sq. ft.
12143 Sq. ft.
Nº 7
10883 Sq. ft.
Nº 8
10518 Sq. ft
9926 Sq. ft.
Nº 10
10482 Sq
Nº 6
14264 Sq. ft.
Nº 5
11211 Sq. ft.
Nº 4
14109 Sq. ft.
Nº 3
17410 Sq. ft
Nº 73
13249 Sq. ft.
Nº 74
14105 Sq. ft.
Nº 75
11434 Sq. ft.
Nº 76
11910 Sq. ft.
PARK LAN
THE GREEN
SHORE RO
PROPOSED
ESPLANADE
PROPOSED PIER
NARRAGANSETT BAY

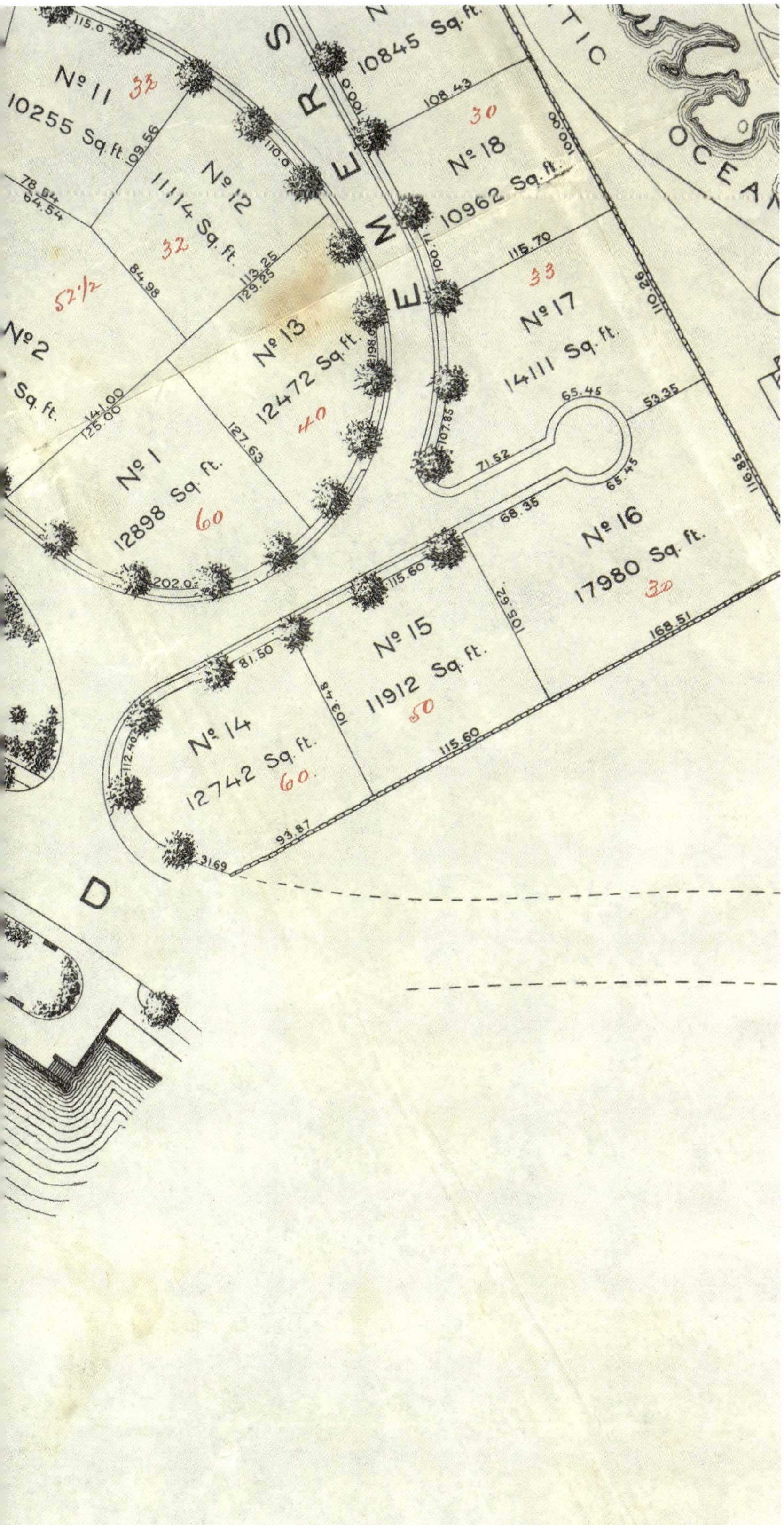

138. Ernest Bowditch. *Plan of the Green at Shoreby Hill* (detail). Plan, 1896. Jamestown Historical Society.

points. Serpentine drives and footpaths lined with trees and shrubs framed open lawns, creating a lush environment of contrast between sun and shade.

The location of Shoreby Hill overlooking the East Passage near the center of town gave it a high visual profile as the land gently rose to the top of a low-lying hill. The art of scene making is at work here. Upon entering the gates, one comes upon a well-planted "green." Curved roads named after colonial Americans of mythic reputation, such as Priscilla, Alden, and Standish, all of *Mayflower* fame, bring one up to a half-moon crescent and then onto a more regular grid of long streets named in honor of literary heroes, Longfellow and Whitman (Fig. 138). Houses set in this picturesque world drew upon the Shingle Style already well established in Jamestown, particularly the cottage (1898) for James Taussig with its shingled facades and gambrel roof. There are also Colonial Revival details to this house: a Classical Revival arch set within the large second-floor gable and Tuscan columns lining the porch. Ephron Catlin's cottage (1898) reveals the same types of fusion of shingled surfaces, prominent gables, and colonial-inspired columns. The C. W. Bailey residence (1899), with one of the most dominant sites in Shoreby Hill, is a full-fledged classical house, its monumental portico of four Ionic columns supporting a pediment, while its curved broken pediment above the front door is a Georgian feature, and the side porches—although decorated with classical balusters and urns on its roof railings—is an entirely modern addition. Thus, it qualifies as the ultimate revival building, freely using historic precedent to make something new.

139. *Shoreby Hill, South Entrance.* Postcard, ca. 1900. Jamestown Historical Society.

140. *Bailey and Parker Cottages.* Postcard, ca. 1900. Sue Maden Postcard Collection. Jamestown Historical Society. The Bailey house is a full-fledged Classical Revival style building, a rarity among the natural shingled picturesque cottages of Jamestown.

Adolphus Knowles also played a major role in Shoreby Hill, building several houses and developing streets.[111] Knowles himself was active from 1900 through the 1930s, and members of his family owned or built several houses in the neighborhood. His siblings and sons acted as carpenters, electricians, and plumbers for many of the projects; his wife was a realtor, managing the rentals and selling many of the properties.[112] He served as president of the Jamestown Town Council, acting town clerk, and general treasurer for Rhode Island. Although he was a director of the Jamestown & Newport Ferry Company, he also owned and operated an excursion boat, the *Sylvan Shore*, making trips between Providence, Rocky Point, and Jamestown, providing ferry services between East Ferry and the Dumplings, and operating a passenger ferry to Newport in opposition to the ferry company.

The paramount role of greenery in Shoreby Hill required the attention of a full-time gardener, a role fulfilled by Albert A. Boone, an English horticulturist and landscape contractor who arrived in America in

141. *Shoreby Hill.* Postcard, ca. 1920. Sue Maden Postcard Collection. Jamestown Historical Society.

142. *James Taussig House.* Photo, 1978. Jamestown Historical Society. A shingled house with Colonial Revival features, notably the Palladian-style arched porch in the second-floor gable.

1890. He started work at Shoreby Hill in 1898, living in the colonial era Greene Farmhouse until 1912, overseeing landscape projects at 47 and 53 Standish Road, and 36 Whittier Road. Boone eventually served as a Rhode Island state senator, Town Council president, and chairman of the Jamestown School Committee and Board of Tax Assessors.[113] In 1912, Boone hired George D. Anthony to build a two-and-a-half-story, L-plan shingled house with cross-gable roof and multiple chimneys on the corner of Holmes Court and Knowles Court. The parcel was part of the original Greene Farm and laid out by Bowditch as small garden lots. Whereas the first houses in Shoreby Hill had been built by Newport contractors, the 1911–31 wave of development was overseen almost exclusively by Jamestown building professionals, real estate developers, contractors, and landscapers, among them George D. Anthony, Adolphus C. Knowles, Albert Boone, and Alonzo Teff.

By the early 1900s, Conanicut's character as pastoral and picturesque appeared to be in good form. Haystacks filled the fields and shingled houses sat contentedly along the coast. It enjoyed golden summers and quiet winters. Architects had produced buildings at one with their settings, drawing upon topography and history as sources of inspiration. Confidence in the stability and serenity of the place seemed assured, as evident in a statement by the Ocean Highlands Company in 1919,

143. *Admirals' Tea.* Photo, 1925. Jamestown Historical Society. Shoreby Hill, along with Dumpling Drive and Ocean Highlands, was popular with naval personnel. Annual teas for active and retired naval officers were held well into the twentieth century.

"Admirals' Tea", Jamestown, R.I.- August 10, 1925

(Rear Admirals, retired, unless otherwise noted. Dates are USNA classes)

Back row-L to R: Captain Todd, USN; Reginald Nicholson, 1873; Bradley Fiske, 1874; William Swinburne, 1866; DeWitt Coffman, 1876; Albert Gleaves, 1877; William B. Bayley:
Front row- L to R: William Marshall, 1871; Yates Stirling, 1863; George C. Remey, 1859; Theodore Jewell, 1865; Joseph Jayne, 1882:

(84th birthday celebration for Rear Admiral Remey, hosted by his daughters, Miss Angelica Remey and Mrs. John Wadleigh at the latter's residence on Shoreby Hill) [Calvert Place]

144. *Casino*. Photo, ca. 1900. Jamestown Historical Society. Built in 1899, the casino functioned as a social club. The term "casino" referred to a pavilion for entertaining, with no connection to gambling. Casinos in nearby Newport and Narragansett, Rhode Island, by the noted firm of McKim, Mead and White in the 1880s had established the fashion for these social buildings, and Jamestown followed suit with this Colonial Revival structure.

> *Jamestown is a conservative and popular summer colony. There are seven hotels at East Ferry, a modern casino, and a country club with golf links, the accessories of a substantial summer colony. Jamestown is popular with United States naval officers and their families during the summer, many of them owning handsome homes… . Jamestown is the coolest, most beautiful and most healthful summer place on Narragansett Bay. Excellent bathing, good boating, sea fishing. Clams, Little Necks, and quahaugs [quohogs] in abundance on the shore. The late William T. Richards, marine artist, testified at a public hearing that the most beautiful marine scenery on the New England coast is in the vicinity of this property.*[114]

The legacy of late nineteenth- and early twentieth-century Jamestown is that of a masterwork of the picturesque view of the world, an ensemble of land and architecture drawing upon a romantic view of the past and an innovative approach to the present. Charles Bevins, J. D. Johnston, Wilson Eyre, Jr., Ernest Bowditch, and other architects and designers each drew upon the aesthetics of their age. The Arts and Crafts emphasis on vernacular forms, natural finishes, rough-hewn surfacing materials, and the appearance of the building rising from its landscape, whatever that terrain and its materials offered, informed the Shingle Style cottages of Conanicut. Queen Anne Revival and Japanesque motifs called upon turned posts and elaborate geometric porch railings, while the Colonial Revival introduced classical pediments, porticos, pillars, and Palladian windows. In Jamestown, the organic quality of these buildings is heightened to a degree seen in very few other places, specifically in the natural way in which houses sit on their places from grassy knoll to cliff. This is the rare and significant place of Conanicut in American cultural and design history, a picturesque place with a storied past for picturesque architecture, each intermingling with the other to produce something extraordinary.

145. *Shoreline Boardwalk*. Photo, ca. 1900. Jamestown Historical Society. The cottages of Shoreby Hill rise in the background above the boardwalk.

CONCLUSION: A PICTURE OF PAST AND PRESENT

IN 1930, RESIDENTS AND VISITORS ALIKE MAY have thought that Jamestown's peace would never be broken by interaction with the outside world. Never assume change will not occur. Buildings rise and fall, but the land has remained a constant. Two world wars and bridges did link the island of Conanicut ever more closely with the mainland. Jamestown Bridge (1940), now known as the Jamestown Verrazzano Bridge, connected the island with South County across the West Passage, while ferries were still necessary to bring passengers across the East Passage to Newport. World War II brought revival to the many strategic points on Conanicut as part of the defenses of Narragansett Bay and to protect the U.S. Atlantic fleet at anchor in Newport (Figs. 146–52).

> *"Because of its island character, Jamestown will always preserve its quiet atmosphere."*
>
> The Book of Rhode Island, 1930

146. *Oliver D. Sprague with Oxen at the Carr Homestead.* Photo, ca. 1920. Jamestown Historical Society. The memory of an agricultural world... a world apart from the nearby mainland.

147. *Henry Armbrust and an Unknown Individual Sitting on a Cannon at Fort Wetherill.* Photo, date unknown but most likely ca. 1914. Jamestown Historical Society.

148. *Casino*. Postcard, ca. 1920. Jamestown Historical Society.

The romantic and picturesque features of Conanicut, so key in its life throughout the nineteenth century, had to step aside and give the stage to twentieth-century realities as Battery 213 commanded the West Passage and Battery Whiting on Beavertail Point guarded the minefields in the East Passage. Fort Burnside, Fort Getty, and Harbor Entrance Control Post also operated in a defense network. Just as in past military conflicts, Conanicut's strategic location in Narragansett Bay brought it to the attention of the U.S. government. With peace came the decommissioning of Jamestown's military installations, and much of the land from Gould, Dutch, and Conanicut Islands was turned into public parks or reserves.

In the 1940s, Catherine Morris Wright settled on Conanicut, purchasing Fox Hill Farm, where ancient Native American remains had been discovered. An author of articles in *Atlantic Monthly* and the *Saturday Evening Post*, and of books such as *Seaweed the Pasture* (1946), she was known as a philanthropist, farmer, and guardian of nature. Her father, Harrison S. Morris, was a director of the Pennsylvania Academy of the Fine Arts, and her grandfather, Joseph Wharton, built Horsehead in Jamestown. History and nature intersected in her efforts to preserve the character of the island, and notably in her giving restrictions to development of her farmland to the Nature Conservancy and donating acreage to create a nature reserve for the Audubon Society. The spirit of this gift harkened back to a well-established appreciation for the land on Conanicut, demonstrated through the ages, and succinctly articulated in 1904, "The village that straggles across the island, following the road from ferry to ferry, is well shaded and pleasant—another object lesson in tree-planting and garden-making,

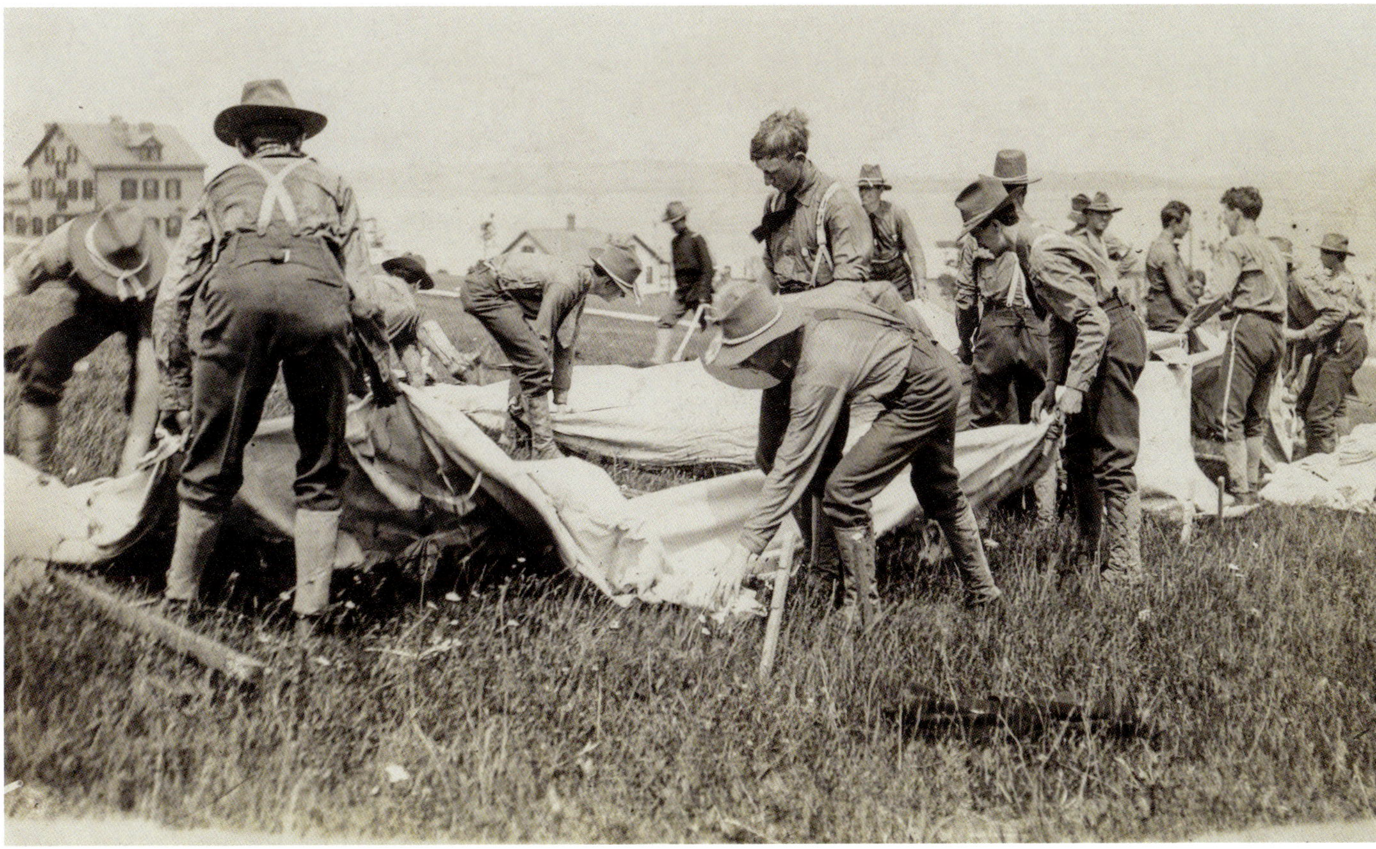

149. *The Rhode Island National Guard Raising Tents at Fort Greble on Dutch Island*. Photo, 1911. Jamestown Historical Society. Fortification of Dutch Island and points on Conanicut formed a critical part of the defense system of Narragansett Bay during World War I and II.

150. *Rhode Island National Guard Camp at Fort Greble*. Photo, 1911. Jamestown Historical Society.

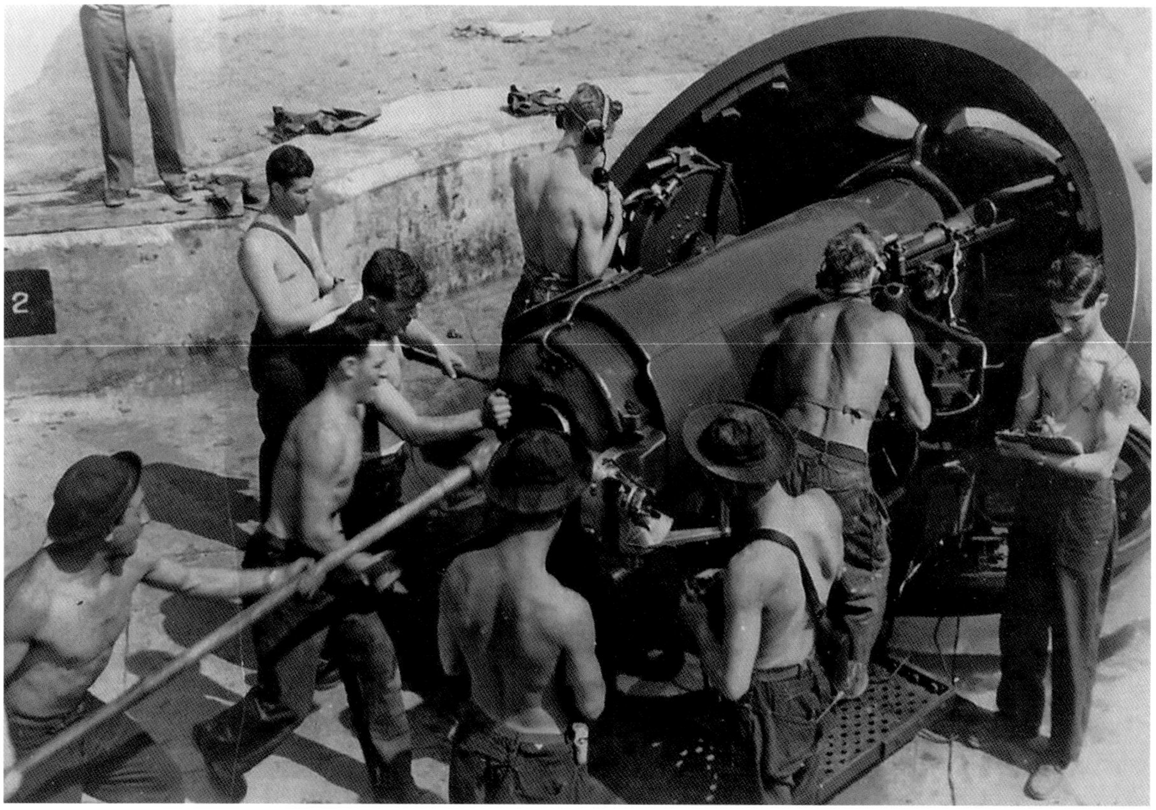

151. *Fort Greble during World War II.* Photo, ca. 1942. Walter K. Schroder Collection. Jamestown Historical Society.

152. *Officers' Houses, Fort Greble*. Photo, ca. 1911. Jamestown Historical Society.

which perhaps will not always be lost upon the people of Rhode Island."[115]

The island was seen by many as an example of centuries-old land management, and relatively well-regulated development, resulting in a place worthy of preservation. As the twentieth century progressed, a new threat loomed over the island. In April 1956, Commerce Oil Refining Corporation, backed by Gulf Oil, presented plans for an 800-acre facility north of Carr Lane. Mary Stearns McGaughan and her husband, Terrence, lived on the Stearns family farm abutting the North End lighthouse at the northern tip of Jamestown. The McGaughans joined with other concerned citizens to form the Jamestown Protective Association in 1957, to oppose the plan. Although the opponents were a minority, they managed to delay the building of the refinery for four years, and, in the end, Gulf Oil withdrew its support for the project.[116] The oil refinery battle made Jamestown residents aware of the need not only to guard against industrial development in the present, but to preserve the land in perpetuity.

Manuel Godena, who had worked for most of his life on small plots or for other farmers, purchased one acre of land and a house in 1907 from John T. Carr. In 1919, he acquired another eight acres near the John F. Weeden farm on the west side of North Main Road. Before he died in 1957, his son Manuel purchased twenty-two acres on the east side of North Main Road from the Carr Homestead Foundation. Commerce Oil bought the surrounding land and bulldozed a lane through his property. The company made an offer for his farm; he refused, stating with regards to their refinery plan, "they're not going to get away with it."[117] Manuel appointed his son, Louis, trustee of his property with power of attorney. Louis transferred the development rights to the Conanicut Island Land Trust, ensuring his grandfather and father's decades of labor would be memorialized and their land preserved, made publicly accessible, and serve as a memorial to the Portuguese and Azorean farmers who labored on the island in the twentieth century. Not only land, but the voices of the Portuguese and Azoreans who settled on the island have been preserved through the efforts of Shirley Teixeira Quattromani, who conducted numerous interviews with residents to ensure their stories would persist into the future in her book *The Portuguese of Conanicut Island: History through Memories, 1895–1980*.[118] In 1969, the land and sea featured prominently again in Jamestown's history with the completion of the bridge over the East Passage from Jamestown to Newport, ending over three hundred years of island isolation (Figs. 153–55). One can say with certainty that the nineteenth century endured in the islands of Narragansett Bay until the late twentieth century due to the lack of bridges. By the 1970s, this centuries-old slumber was over. Conanicut is a destination for some, and a transit point for most as traffic races back and forth to Newport in the east and the mainland in the west.

153. *Jamestown Bridge Construction*. Photo, 1939. Harold Sherman Collection. Jamestown Historical Society.

154. *Jamestown Bridge, Worker*. Jamestown Historical Society.

155. *Jamestown Bridge Opening: Souvenir Program*, 1940. Jamestown Historical Society.

Although connected to the mainland, there still appears to be an air of quiet on Conanicut, the product of its location and preservation efforts. The island offers an age-old lesson in how topography, scenery, history, and buildings, when working in concert, can produce something of timeless value, an eternal paradise, if you will. Change is inevitable; new buildings appear. The island still retains its natural assets, which have proven over the centuries to be the foundation of its enduring appeal. The rocky coastline remains indomitable, the historic windmill still sits atop its hill, and the atmosphere of Conanicut is immortalized in the paintings of William Trost Richards, in photographs, and in the written accounts of so many witnesses through time, who recorded, interpreted, celebrated, and protected the dumplings, the coves, the sheep, the haystacks, and the old shingled houses for posterity: the pastoral and picturesque preserved in memory, for the present and the future (Figs. 156–58).

> *If imagination can add to the present beauty of this great labyrinth of waters the charm of that abundant verdure described by navigators and historians, the picture will be one of unexampled loveliness… . Scattered about the bay a few capes, islands, and estuaries bear the names of early settlers… . Some of the place names are Indian, and many of them are mere navigator's names, handed down from generation to generation.*[119]

156. William Trost Richards. *The Cottrell Farm, Conanicut Island.* Watercolor and Chinese white on paper, 1884. Courtesy of the Pennsylvania Academy of the Fine Arts. Gift of Dorrance H. Hamilton in memory of Samuel M. V. Hamilton.

Following pages:
157. William Trost Richards. *Horsehead, Conanicut Island* (sketch). Oil on canvas board, late 19th century. Pennsylvania Academy of the Fine Arts.

158. William Trost Richards. *Dumplings at Twilight*. Watercolor and Chinese white on paper, 1883. Courtesy of the Pennsylvania Academy of the Fine Arts. Gift of Dorrance H. Hamilton in memory of Samuel M. V. Hamilton.

My father wrote me a letter—My father,
scholarly, indolent, strong,
Teaching Greek better
Than high-school students repay—
Teaching Greek in the winter, but all summer long
Sailing a yawl in Narragansett Bay;
Happier perhaps when I was away,
Free of an anxious daughter,
He could sail blue water
Day after day,
Beyond Brenton Reef Lightship, and Beavertail,
Past Cuttyhunk to catch a gale
Off the Cape, while he thought of Hellas and Troy,
Chanting with joy

Alice Duer Miller, *The White Cliffs*, 1940

ENDNOTES

1 James W. Skehan et al., *The Mississippian and Pennsylvanian (Carboniferous) Systems in the United States – Massachusetts, Rhode Island and Maine*, U.S. Geological Survey Professional Paper 1110 (Washington, DC: United States Government Printing Office, 1979), https://www.ngs.noaa.gov/desc_reports/T10500.PDF.

2 William Scranton Simmons, *Cautantowwit's House: An Indian Burial Ground on the Island of Conanicut in Narragansett Bay* (Providence, R.I.: Brown University Press, 1970).

3 Brian Holt Hawthorne, "Ecological Restoration of Fire-Maintained Oak Woodlands in Massachusetts," Master's thesis, University of Massachusetts, 2004.

4 Rhode Island Historical Preservation & Heritage Commission, *Historic and Architectural Resources of Jamestown, Rhode Island* (Providence: Rhode Island Historical Preservation & Heritage Commission, 1995), p. 6.

5 Lawrence C. Wroth, *The Voyages of Giovanni da Verrazzano, 1524–1528* (New Haven, CT: Yale University Press, 1970).

6 According to Wroth (ibid., p. 232), Verrazzano annotated his manuscript at this point: "which we called 'La Petra Viva,' on account of both the nature of the stone and the family of a gentlewoman; on the right side of the harbor mouth there is a promontory which we called Jovius Promontory."

7 Wroth, *Voyages of Giovanni da Verrazzano*, pp. 133–34.

8 Ibid.

9 Lucianne Lavin, ed., *Dutch and Indigenous Communities in Seventeenth-Century Northeastern North America: What Archaeology, History, and Indigenous Oral Traditions Teach Us about Their Intercultural Relationships* (Albany: State University of New York, 2021).

10 Simmons, *Cautantowwit's House*, p. 5. There is a second archeological site on the island of significance, the West Ferry Site, which was excavated by William Scranton Simmons in 1966. Prior to the investigation, it is said that men digging on the site "uncovered the grave of a 'chief' who was said to have lain facing east with his head set upon a large square of sheet brass and with a castellated pot and iron ax by his side" (ibid., p. 8). The burials discovered by Simmons and the local Jamestown population proved to be some of the richest ever found in Rhode Island, including Prehistoric and Narragansett examples. It is said that the Archaic period burials found directly next to those of the much later Narragansett tribal ones could have been unknown to the Narragansetts.

11 First Newport Town Meeting, 1639, Newport Town Records Collection, Rhode Island Historical Society (hereafter RIHS).

12 Newport Land Evidence Book, no. 1, p. 6, City of Newport Property Records.

13 1657 Conanicut Land Agreement, Jamestown Historical Society, Jamestown, Rhode Island (hereafter JHS).

14 Ibid. Benedict Arnold, infamous as a traitor to the cause of independence during the American Revolution, was a descendant of the prominent Arnold family of colonial Rhode Island.

15 W. L. Watson, *History of Jamestown on Conanicut Island in the State of Rhode Island* (Providence, R.I.: John F. Greene, 1949), p. 7.

16 Ibid., p. 12.

17 Ibid., p. 14. The town was incorporated on November 4, 1678, and the first town meeting was held in April 1679.

18 1705 Town Record, May 1, 1705, signed by William Sanford, town clerk, RIHS.

19 The 1730 and 1775 censuses and the 1709 town survey are detailed in Virginia D. Harrington and Evarts B. Greene, *American Population before the Federal Census of 1790* (New York: Columbia University Press, 1932).

20 James N. Arnold, *The Life and Times of Benedict Arnold: First Governor of Rhode Island under the Charter* (Newport, R.I.: Mercury Publishing Company, 1901).

21 Watson, *History of Jamestown*, p. 19.

22 Ibid., pp. 19–21.

23 Ibid., p. 19.

24 Damaris Fowler, Manumission Record of Jane, May 30, 1775. Society of Friends Records, Volume 821, Collection of the Newport Historical Society (hereafter NHS).

25 Watson, *History of Jamestown*, p. 16.

26 Ibid.

27 Will of Joseph Greene, November 5, 1839, JHS, A2019.1033.002.

28 Plan of the Greene Farm in Jamestown on the land of Conanicut, R.I., surveyed and drawn by direction of Thomas P. Nichols, Israel Buffington Francis Taylor, Trustees, by J. R. Hodges C. Eng., 1861, JHS, A2006.354.001.

29 Newport Friends meeting minutes of December 24, 1684, NHS.

30 Watson, *History of Jamestown*, p. 73.

31 Land Evidence Records for 1710, JHS.

32 Damage recorded in Newport Friends minutes on May 28, 1776; rebuilding of meeting house recorded in Newport Friends minutes on September 26, 1786.

33 Watson, *History of Jamestown*, p. 65.

34 Ibid., p. 67.

35 Ibid., p. 101.

36 Ibid. No relation to Thomas Paine who gained renown for publishing *Common Sense* (1776).

37 Ibid., p. 93 (will of 1693/94).

38 Norman Isham dated the house to the late 1600s or early 1700s.

39 Watson, *History of Jamestown*, pp. 91–93.

40 Ibid., p. 24.

41 *The Literary Diary of Ezra Stiles*, ed. Franklin Bowditch Dexter (New York: Charles Scribner's Sons, 1901), vol. 1, p. 642. See also the account of the burning of Jamestown in the *Providence Gazette*, December 16, 1775.

42 Ibid.

43 Harrington and Greene, *American Population before the Federal Census of 1790*, census records for 1777.

44 *A Topographical Chart of the Bay of Narraganset in the Province of New England*, drawn by Charles Blaskowitz, published by William Faden. There is a copy of the map in the Library of Congress.

45 Ibid.

46 *Diary of Frederick Mackenzie*, ed. Allen French (Cambridge, MA: Harvard University Press, 1930), vol. 1, p. 182.

47 "The Rhode Island 1777 Military Census," transcribed by Mildred Chamberlain, published under the direction of the Rhode Island Genealogical Society in 1985; a three-page photocopy from the book includes the 1777 Military Census of Jamestown, R.I.

48 Family reminiscences as retold by Mary Louise Weeden, https://www.jamestownpress.com/articles/jamestown-historical-society-feature-12/.

49 Watson, *History of Jamestown*, p. 39.

50 Richard M. Bayles, ed., *History of Newport County, Rhode Island, from the year 1638 to the year 1887, including the settlement of its towns, and their subsequent progress* (New York: L. E. Preston & Co., 1888).

51 MSS 201 Jamestown Town Records, RIHS, Box 1 of 1, MSS 201 B1 F4, Petition to the General Assembly concerning the tax bill of July 20, 1784.

52 "A List of the Polls and Estates Real and Personal of the Proprietors and Inhabitants of the Town of Jamestown in the State of Rhode Island as taken by the Subscribers in Pursuant to an Act of the General Assembly passed at their session," 1783, Jamestown Town Records and Probate, vol. 2, p. 185.

53 Town of Jamestown Proprietor Records, Births, Deaths, and Marriages, vol. 1, 1672–1859.

54 Newport Town Council, September 8, 1819 (Book 2006).

55 Handwritten account information from the town of Jamestown to John Remington, October 19, 1819, JHS, T2007.031.019.

56 "1790 Federal Census Newport County, Rhode Island," abstracted by Lorraine H. Robinson from public records, edited and formatted by Maggie Stewart, http://files.usgwarchives.net/ri/newport/census/1790/pg296.txt.

57 Rosemary Enright, *Jamestown: A History of Narragansett Bay's Island Town* (Jamestown, R.I.: Jamestown Historical Society, 2010), p. 52.

58 Ibid.

59 Ibid., p. 57.

60 Ibid., p. 53.

61 Edgar Mayhew Bacon, *Narragansett Bay: Its Historic and Romantic Associations and Picturesque Setting* (New York and London: G. P. Putnam's Sons, 1904), p. 56.

62 Virginia Galvin Covell, "A Critical Examination of the Town and Country Club of Newport, Rhode Island," Master's thesis, University of Rhode Island, 1964, p. 3.

63 William H. Jordy et al., "Conanicut Park", in *SAH Archipedia*, ed. Gabrielle Esperdy and Karen Kingsley (Charlottesville: University of Virginia Press, 2012–), http://sah-archipedia.org/buildings/RI-01-JA5.

64 J. R. Cole, "Town of Jamestown," in Bayles, *History of Newport County*, pp. 736–44.

65 Jordy, "Conanicut Park."

66 Mariana M. Tallman, *Pleasant Places in Rhode Island, and How to Reach Them* (Providence, R.I.: The Providence Journal Company, 1893), p. 56.

67 Ibid., p. 57.

68 Ibid., p. 57.

69 Ibid., p. 58.

70 Ibid., p. 59.

71 *Providence Journal*, 1887.

72 Rhode Island Historical Preservation & Heritage Commission, *Historic and Architectural Resources of Jamestown.*

73 Linda S. Ferber, "An American Pre-Raphaelite in New York: William Trost Richards," *Archives of American Art Journal* 47, nos. 1/2 (2008), pp. 4–15.

74 Lawrence Wodehouse, "'New Path' and the American Pre-Raphaelite Brotherhood," *Art Journal* 25, no. 4 (1966), pp. 351–54.

75 Thomas Wentworth Higginson, *Oldport Days* (Boston: James R. Osgood and Company, 1873), p. 65.

76 W. Ross Yates, *Joseph Wharton: Quaker Industrial Pioneer* (Bethlehem, PA: Lehigh University Press, 1987), p. 238.

77 "Joseph Wharton is Dead: Prominent Ironmaker Expires at Home in Philadelphia," *New York Times*, January 12, 1909.

78 Letter of July 22, 1883, from Deborah Fisher Wharton to her son Joseph Wharton regarding the construction of Horsehead, JHS, Ephemera Folder: Houses, 19th Century, Summer Homes 6.

79 "Jamestown," *Newport Mercury*, June 30, 1888, Section 1, p. 8.

80 "The Big Statue Arrives", *New York Tribune*, June 18, 1885.

81 "Capt. Selfridge's Acquittal," *New York Times*, June 18, 1888, p. 4.

82 Thomas O. Selfridge, Jr., *What Finer Tradition: The Memoirs of Thomas O. Selfridge, Jr., Rear Admiral, U.S.N.*, 1924.

83 Ibid.

84 According to the *Newport Daily News* of September 13, 1895, the house became a tea house around 1910, T. F. Kennedy's summer residence in 1926, was taken for Fort Burnside in 1941, and accidently destroyed by fire in 1942.

85 "Wilson Eyre, Jr.," *Philadelphia Architects and Buildings*, https://www.philadelphiabuildings.org/pab/app/ar_display.cfm/25852.

86 James C. Buttrick, "So Who Was Charles Bevins?," Occasional Paper #1, JHS, 2002. Bevins eventually settled at Meadowsweet Farm in Jamestown and lived there until 1925.

87 George William Sheldon, *Artistic Country-Seats: Types of Recent American Villa and Cottage Architecture, with Instances of Country Club-Houses* (New York: Da Capo Press, 1979) and Vincent Scully, *The Shingle Style and the Stick Style: Architectural Theory and Design from Richardson to the Origins of Wright* (New Haven and New London: Yale University Press, 1971).

88 Buttrick, "So Who Was Charles Bevins?"

89 "The Palace Cottages of Newport," *Munsey's Magazine*, September 1897.

90 Buttrick, "So Who Was Charles Bevins?" James Buttrick has identified over forty buildings attributed to Charles Bevins based on architectural and stylistic analysis.

91 William H. Jordy and Christopher P. Monkhouse, *Buildings on Paper: Rhode Island Architectural Drawings, 1825–1945* (Providence: Rhode Island School of Design, 1982), p. 220.

92 William H. Jordy et al., "J. S. Lovering Wharton House (Clingstone)," in *SAH Archipedia*, ed. Gabrielle Esperdy and Karen Kingsley (Charlottesville University of Virginia Press, 2012–), http://sah-archipedia.org/buildings/RI-01-JA29.

See also John Dixon Johnston. Clingstone House—North Elevation. Newport, RI. n.d.. Ink on paper. ARCHITECTURAL DRAWING. Graphics—Architectural Drawings—Tube 60—AD575. John Dixon Johnston. Clingstone House—West

Elevation. Newport, RI. n.d.. Ink on paper. ARCHITECTURAL DRAWING. Graphics—Architectural Drawings—Tube 60—AD577. John Dixon Johnston. Clingstone House—First Floor Floor Plan. Newport, RI. n.d.. Ink on paper. ARCHITECTURAL DRAWING. Graphics—Architectural Drawings—Tube 60—AD575.

93 Juanita Marie Holland and Corrine Jennings, *Edward Mitchell Bannister, 1828–1901* (New York: Kenkeleba House, 1992).

94 George Leland Miner, William Chesley Worthington, and Louis D. Atwood, *Providence Art Club, 1880–2005* (Providence, R.I.: Providence Art Club), pp. 127, 132.

95 Robert S. Peabody, "Georgian Houses of New England," *American Architect and Building News* 2 (October 20, 1877), p. 338. Peabody was an important early advocate for colonial architecture. See also Jordy and Monkhouse, *Buildings on Paper*.

96 McKim Portfolio, NHS.

97 "Captain Thomas Paine House: Handout from Anne W. Baker Notes," *Documentation* 126 (May 2022), https://docs.rwu.edu/cgi/viewcontent.cgi?article=1125&context=baker_documentation.

98 From Harry Carr's column on the Carr Homestead in the *Los Angeles Times*, 1925.

99 W. L. Watson, *The House of Carr: A Historical Sketch of the Carr Family from 1490 to 1926, written in observance of the one hundred and fiftieth anniversary of the construction of the Carr Homestead in 1776* (Providence, R.I., 1926).

100 Ibid.

101 Enright, *Jamestown*, p. 112.

102 *The Homes of Our Forefathers, being a selection of the oldest and most interesting buildings, historic houses, and noted places in Rhode Island and Connecticut, from the original drawings made on the spot by Edwin Whitefield* (Boston: Whitefield and Crocker), 1882.

103 Emily DeFazio, "'That Awful Spectacle': Masking the City-by-the-Sea's Piratical Past," blog post, July 3, 2024, https://newporthistory.org/that-awful-spectacle-masking-the-city-by-the-seas-piratical-past/.

104 Sarah Kidd, letter dated July 18, 1699, The National Archives.

105 Gloria Merchant, *Pirates of Colonial Newport* (Charleston, S.C.: The History Press, 2014), p. 38.

106 Ibid.

107 Bacon, *Narragansett Bay*, p. 58.

108 Rhode Island Historical Preservation & Heritage Commission, *Historic and Architectural Resources of Jamestown*.

109 National Register of Historic Places, July 28, 2011.

110 Ernest Bowditch, "Office Work-Personalities II," no. 5, Bowditch Family Papers, The Peabody Essex Institute Museum, Salem, MA. Also see *Pioneers of American Landscape Design* and G. M. Hopkins, *City Atlas of Newport*, 1883 and *Newport Atlas*, 1895.

111 Douglas, Fowler, Swinburne, and Harriet Streets. Sue Maden and Rosemary Enright, *The Jamestown Press*, July 23, 2023.

112 National Register of Historic Places, July 28, 2011.

113 Ibid.

114 Ocean Highlands Company liquidation sale brochure, 1919, JHS.

115 Bacon, *Narragansett Bay*, p. 56.

116 Mary Stearns McGaughan and Terence F. McGaughan, *Dismissed with Prejudice: The Epic Battle against Construction of an Oil Refinery in Jamestown, Rhode Island* (Jamestown, R.I.: Jamestown Historical Society, 1994).

117 Peter Fay for *The Jamestown Press* on August 25, 2022.

118 Shirley Teixeira Quattromani and Catherine Morris Wright, eds., *The Portuguese of Conanicut Island: History through Memories, 1895–1980* (Jamestown, R.I.: Philomenian Library, 1980).

119 Bacon, *Narragansett Bay*, p. 13.

SELECTED BIBLIOGRAPHY

DIRECTORIES, MAPS, AND TOWN RECORDS:

Bryant, William Cullen, ed. *Picturesque America; or, The Land We Live In: A delineation in pen and pencil of the mountains, rivers, lakes, forests, water-falls, shores, cañons, valleys, cities, and other picturesque features of our country, with illustrations on steel and wood, by eminent American artists*. Volume 1. New York: D. Appleton Company, 1872.

C. DeWitt White Company. *Jamestown and New Shoreham Directory*. Providence: C. DeWitt White Company, 1912, 1915, 1918, 1920, 1922–31, 1936, 1937, and 1948.

Jamestown Land Company. *Shoreby Hill, Jamestown, RI*. Map and sales brochure. Jamestown, R.I.: Jamestown Land Company, 1896.

Newport Daily News (September 1896–October 1898).

Newport Journal (September 1895–November 1899).

Jamestown Tax Assessor. Annual Tax Lists. Jamestown, R.I., 1891–2010.

Jamestown Building Department. Building Permit Records. Jamestown, R.I., 1905–2010.

Jamestown Town Clerk. Land Evidence Records. Jamestown, R.I., 1860–2010.

Sanborn Map Company. Jamestown, Rhode Island maps (1903, 1911, 1921, 1941). New York: Sanborn Map Company, 1903–41.

Social Index Publishing Company. *Newport Social Index* (1909–1931). Newport: Social Index Publishing Company.

BOOKS AND ARTICLES

Buttrick, James C., and Jamestown Historical Society. *Jamestown* (Images of America Series). Portsmouth, N.H.: Arcadia Publishing, 2003.

Delude, Elizabeth Mary. "Jamestown, Rhode Island: A Nineteenth Century Resort and Shoreby Hill, A Resort Suburb." Master's thesis, Columbia University, 1986.

Enright, Rosemary, and Sue Maden. *Jamestown: A History of Narragansett Bay's Island Town*. Jamestown, R.I.: Jamestown Historical Society, 2010.

Frazier, A., ed. *Club, Bench, Bar, and Professional Life: A Journal for Club Men and Women*. Providence, 1896.

Hamilton, Esley. "Shoreby Hill: A St. Louis Colony in Rhode Island." *The Society of Architectural Historians, Missouri Valley Chapter Newsletter* 10, no. 2A (Summer 2004), pp. 1–3.

Howard, John H. *100 Years in Jamestown: From Destination Resort to Bedroom Town*. Jamestown, R.I.: Jamestown Historical Society, 2000.

Jordy, William H. *Buildings of Rhode Island*. New York: Oxford University Press, 2004.

Maden, Sue. *The Building Boom in Jamestown, Rhode Island, 1926–1931*. Jamestown, R.I.: West Ferry Press, 2004.

Murphy, Kevin D. "Ernest W. Bowditch and the Practice of Landscape Architecture." In *Essex Institute Historical Collections*, Volume 125, pp. 162–76. Salem, M.A.: Essex Institute, 1989.

Rhode Island Historical Preservation & Heritage Commission. *Historical and Architectural Resources of Jamestown, Rhode Island*. Providence: Rhode Island Historical Preservation & Heritage Commission, 1995. Also available online at https://preservation.ri.gov/sites/g/files/xkgbur406/files/pdfs_zips_downloads/survey_pdfs/jamestown.pdf

ONLINE RESOURCES

https://www.nps.gov/jame/learn/historyculture/upload/African%20Americans%20on%20Jamestown%20Island.pdf

https://jamestownhistoricalsociety.catalogaccess.com/archives/49031

https://siris-artinventories.si.edu/ipac20/ipac.jsp?uri=full=3100001~!345139!

INDEX

IMAGE CREDITS

Jamestown Historical Society
Library of Congress
Pennsylvania Academy of the Fine Arts
Rhode Island Historical Society

John R. Tschirch is an award-winning architectural historian and Honorary Member of the Garden Club of America. He has written and lectured widely on architecture and landscapes across the globe and advises on the preservation of historic sites. His publications on Rhode Island address the region's significant architectural and artistic heritage.

David E. Weisman is a native Rhode Islander who, in addition to successful careers in law and business, is a recognized collector of nineteenth- and twentieth-century French art and a board member of the National Archives Foundation as well as current Chairman of the Board of Directors of FINCA International in Washington, D.C. With Jacqueline E. Michel, he founded the Weisman & Michel Collection of paintings and works of art focused on artists whose works reflect the avant-garde spirit of Montmartre during the Belle Époque.

Duck Cove
Plumb-beach Pt.
Fox Island
Coles Ledge and Point
Cole Harbour
North Ferry
CONNONICUT
ISLAND
West Ferry
Cranston's Cove
GOULD ISLAND
Coddington's Point
Cove
Bishops Rock
Taylors Point
COASTERS HARBOUR ISLAND
Blue Rock
DUTCH ISLAND
Great Creek
West Ferry
East Ferry
ROSE ISLAND
Mr. Malbone Battery
Dyers Point
Foxhill Cove
South Ferry
Beaver Head
Foxhill
GOAT ISLAND
Fort
Long Wharf
Cove
Dumpling Rocks
Brenton's Point
Battery
Rock
Ledge
Brentons Cove
Mackerel Cove
Pond
Mr. Jahleel Brenton
the Bonnet
Castle Hill
Mr. James Brenton
Mr. John Collins
Whale Rock
Light House
Beaver Tail
Old Newtown Rock
Brentons Reef
Prices Neck
Gooseberry Island
Rock